IRRITATING

the ones you Love

IRRITATING
the ones you *Love*

The Down and Dirty Guide
to Better Relationships

Dr. Jeff Auerbach

PLAIN SIGHT PUBLISHING
An imprint of Cedar Fort, Inc.
Springville, Utah

The opinions and views expressed in this publication belong solely to the author and do not necessarily represent the opinions or views of Cedar Fort, Inc. Permission for the use of sources, graphics, and photos is also solely the responsibility of the author.

ISBN 13: 978-1-55517-604-4

Published by Plain Sight Publishing, an imprint of Cedar Fort, Inc.
2373 W. 700 S., Springville, UT 84663
Distributed by Cedar Fort, Inc., www.cedarfort.com

The Library of Congress has cataloged the 2002 edition as follows:

Auerbach, Jeff, 1964-
  Irritating the ones you love : the down and dirty guide to better
relationships / by Jeff Auerbach.
      p. cm.
  ISBN 1-55517-604-6 (pbk. : alk. paper)
  1. Interpersonal relations. 2. Man-woman relationships. 3. Couples.
4. Mate selection. 5. Love. I. Title.
  HM1106 .A94 2002
  306.7--dc21

                                        2002000399

Cover design by Angela R. Decker
Cover design © 2013 by Lyle Mortimer
Typeset by Kristin Nelson

Printed in the United States of America

10 9 8 7 6

Printed on acid-free paper

Contents

Introduction

Irritating the Ones You Love is intended to be a quick read for busy people (it is the "down-and-dirty guide to relationships"). Clearly, in order to remedy what doesn't work about relationships, we must first identify the things about them that are "wrong." While much of the book focuses on these aspects, it also recognizes just how beautiful relationships can be when they work well. The overriding goal of the book is to help people improve their relationships in a real and meaningful way. If you're already in a great one, this book can give you tools to make it even better, and if you're not, it can help you to find what you're looking for.

It offers practical, thought-provoking, and bottom line information about common barriers to happy and successful relationships. It's built on one primary premise: that which we are not aware of, we are powerless to control. Awareness is the key to control, just as control is the key to change. The text also provides answers to some seemingly "unanswerable" relationship questions, including:

1. Why do we often seem to keep having the same "dysfunctional" relationship(s) over and over again, but with different people?

2. Why do couples (even those who have a great relationship overall) tend to have the same two or three arguments over and over?

3. Why is it that people often stay in relationships that are unhappy or destructive far longer than would seem practical?

4. What causes two people who appear to be poorly matched to be drawn together and pursue a relationship in the first place?

5. Why are people frequently drawn to those who seem to hurt

them, while they often reject others who treat them well and appear to be a "catch"?

6. Why do people make choices regarding relationships that are so obviously "wrong" that everyone else can see it (e.g., friends, family) except the person/people involved?

As you read this book and discover that there are actually clear and systematic (but "invisible") *patterns* to why people do what they do, you will most likely find yourself reflecting on your own relationship history and saying, "No wonder!" While some of the themes in this book may be generally familiar, there are many crucial aspects that are unique. The biggest of these is that all relationships actually consist of a "dual reality", meaning that they are always operating on two levels at the same time: visible and invisible. Many helpful books have been written about how to make better choices and improve communication with respect to the visible layer. *Irritating the Ones You Love* draws special attention to the "invisible" layer. If it's invisible, you can't avoid it; if you can see it, you can *do* something about it.

In reading this text, you will be able to illuminate and understand things about your own relationships, choices, and reactions that you may have been previously unable to explain, things about your own behavior that just didn't seem to "make sense," even to you. In addition, as you become aware of this typically "hidden" information, you will end up knowing and understanding things about the relationship process that most other people just wouldn't be aware of. This book introduces an extremely powerful, original model called "The Three Jars Technique." Your Three "Jars" (i.e., "buttons" or issues) provides you with a deeply revealing blueprint of yourself and your partner (or prospective partner). With three clear, simple labels (such as fairness, control, or guilt), you will be able to understand virtually any situation in your life that you would consider to be unwanted or undesirable. The tools that are presented are systematic, concrete, and user-friendly, and will not only help you to deal more effectively with people in your romantic relationships, but with those in your everyday life as well.

Readers will vary in the way that *Irritating the Ones You Love* applies to them and their own relationship(s). As discussed in detail in the text, all couples are part of one "relationship continuum," which includes those marked by unhappiness and ongoing strife, those that are generally "pretty good" but which are somewhat lacking vitality and mutual satisfaction, and those that most people would aspire to, in which both partner's experiences are vastly more positive and rewarding than they are hurtful or undesirable. If you've already got a great relationship, then this text offers information to help you with some of the "fine tuning," including tools that will assist you in deepening your understanding of one another. For those fortunate enough to fall into this category, you may find that the third chapter ("How to Choose the Right One") won't apply as much to you, given that your search for a partner will already have been completed. For others still in the process of seeking their "true love," or trying to determine whether their current relationship fits this description, the material in this chapter will be extremely relevant and useful.

Hopefully, all readers will find this book to be informative, practical, and easy to read. Every example in the book is authentic (with appropriate steps taken for confidentiality). You may find these stories especially powerful because they *are* based on real people's real experiences—and you may see a piece of yourself (or a partner, past or present) in them. As I speak with couples, groups, and organizations about this topic, there's an expression that I'm especially fond of using: "Most arguments in relationships are caused by coffee makers and donuts." By the time you get through most of this book, you'll know what I mean.

Author's Note

The writing of this book has been an utterly amazing experience for me personally. As people who know me can attest, I've never been one to enjoy "homework" and other academic tasks. As a result, the writing process is one that tends to be rather undesirable for me. In this case, however, it truly became a "labor of love."

There are a number of people I wish to thank and express deep gratitude to for the vast opportunities, wisdom, and guidance that they have offered me along the way. First, from a professional standpoint, there have been several individuals who have been particularly influential in my understanding of human beings and relationships. They include Dr. M. Scott Peck, who helped to launch me on my "road" of personal growth; Dr. Sigmund Freud, whose imprint can be found in virtually every foundation of human psychology, and whose concepts of repetition and transference continue to be highly relevant; Dr. Leon Festinger and his far-reaching Cognitive Dissonance Theory; Dr. Harville Hendricks, who helped to plant a seed in my mind about the repetition of romantic relationships; and Dr. Jerry Skillings, who has been a valued friend, mentor, and supporter throughout my career.

I owe an infinite debt of gratitude to my wonderful clients, family, friends, and acquaintances, whose wealth of wisdom and experience have informed this process in ways that cannot be measured. And finally, to my previous girlfriends and significant others, who all, in their own unique way, contributed to my knowledge, growth, and development, both as a person and as a partner. I cannot adequately express how much I appreciate their enhancement of my own relationship path.

Many paradoxes can be found throughout the content of this work. It is written in a manner that is often "reductionistic," boiling large volumes of information down to simple, concrete, and usable concepts. At the same time, it recognizes how much "gray" there is in the human condition; that reality is often the product of many (often conflicting) dynamics all swirled together. As human beings, we are capable of experiencing a wide spectrum of thoughts and feelings. To effectively work on or understand a particular situation, sometimes it is practical to concentrate on certain *parts* of that spectrum more than others. For the record, this is not meant to imply a lack of recognition of the fuller spectrum (for example, although there may be many painful or upsetting aspects of relationships, they also offer an almost infinite potential to generate excitement, joy, and meaning).

One of the most challenging aspects of any effort to better understand and improve our relationships is that we must examine them, and the people involved, more closely. Talk about a double-edged sword! On one hand, we are invested in having a positive view of that person—and yet, there may be things that are not as positive as we'd like them to be (given that, of course, *everyone* has their "quirks"). But it's not an all or nothing situation, one in which all that's desirable is discounted by the presence of anything that's not, any more than that which is undesirable can be ignored because of the presence of positive aspects. We as humans tend to be rather uncomfortable dealing with gray; feelings are much easier to tolerate when they're black and white, when we can know exactly where we stand. But, as you already know, that's not the nature of life. We are often forced to reconcile more than one set of feelings for the same situation or person, and that tends to be inherently uncomfortable.

What I'd like to particularly emphasize is that, because this is a book about relationships, it means looking more closely at important people in your life (e.g., yourself, your partner, and your family). In order to make healthy, positive changes, we must often first see that which isn't so positive. **Looking at, feeling, discussing, or thinking of uncomplimentary things about someone you love is not a sin, a crime, or a violation of any universal law.** It doesn't mean you don't love them, care about them, or feel lucky to have them in your life—and you need not feel guilty about it. It's all part of what it means to have a real relationship. This applies to partners, parents, and anyone else in our lives.

For example, while in the final process of completing this book, I got a new kitten. She was everything that you could possibly want in a kitten—extremely affectionate, curious, energetic, and playful. On the other hand, she was also everything that can be a hassle about owning a pet—extremely affectionate, curious, energetic, and playful (e.g., won't leave you alone, gets into everything, knocks over and tears up trash, etc.). Such is the dual reality of all relationships. Overall, she's a joy to have around, and I wouldn't trade her, with all of her unique qualities, for any other animal in the world. On the other hand, sometimes I could do without some of her more *annoying* unique qualities. If this is true for relationships with pets, how much messier and more complicated can our feelings be toward *people*? This inherent level of imperfection comes with the package of human relationships. The more we can see them and understand them for what they are (hopefully without judgment), the more fully satisfying they can be. Enjoy.

Chapter One

Invisible Love

"They" say that love is blind; they don't tell us why. "They" say that opposites attract, but they don't tell us how. "They" don't even know how right they are. Most people would very much like to be in a happy, stable relationship. As most of us know, this is often easier said than done. On the surface, it seems that it should be easy; after all, there are few feelings more natural and joyful than falling in love. But below the surface, the mating process—and human beings—are more complicated.

One of the things that makes this true for romantic relationships is that there are some, for lack of a better word, "secrets" about how the process works. In some ways love isn't even always romantic. The basic concepts about relationships that are generally accepted, the ones that we buy into as a society, are, in many important ways, untrue. Some people are aware of this misinformation; in fact, it's in the cultural consciousness enough to be discussed on television programs and in movies. Yet, for the vast majority of people in this country and throughout the world (relationship professionals included), the true nature of the bonds and cycles that influence relationships remains a mystery.

Common Misconceptions About "Love"

The information presented here may seem inconsistent with what you've always been taught, because many of the ideas that we use to guide us, those that we hear in conversations with friends and relatives, and see represented in movies and on television, are largely inaccurate. This is because that body of information tends to miss a vitally important aspect of the process by which two people are drawn together. Love is a very complex phenomenon, and as such, operates on a number of powerful levels at the same time. For the sake of discussion, these can be divided into five broad categories:

1. **romantic** (the blissful feeling of being "in love" with someone)
2. **sexual** (compatible appetites, styles, and satisfaction)
3. **practical** (the "business" aspect of a partnership and the ability to cooperate)
4. **companionship** (the pleasure of spending time with a person whose company you enjoy)
6. **growth** (the willingness to mutually struggle with issues and conflict)

Each of these categories are highly complex in and of themselves, and therefore involve multiple dimensions. For instance, the romantic aspect, which contains much of what we traditionally associate with the feeling of "falling in love," is a tremendously pleasant and rewarding experience. The very fact that we're able to find another human being with whom we're able to share such a sense of joy and excitement has almost a "magical" quality to it. It requires an amazing combination of ingredients—the right place at the right time, luck, opportunity, common interests and styles—that it's hard to imagine there aren't outside influences at work.

Clearly, this wonderful feeling of being "in love" is one of the major forces that fuels our motivation to seek relationships in the first place. As most people have experienced, the state of being in love does not necessarily remain constant. Often, when time progresses and some of the initial luster of those feelings wears off a bit, other aspects of the person, perhaps less desirable ones, may emerge. Even though they may be happy with their relationship overall, couples may find that there are certain issues that they seem to consistently get irritated about. Over the years of working with thousands of clients, I've observed that this phenomenon is no accident (as have many other therapists); that, in fact, it's part of a very systematic and widespread relationship **pattern**.

One of the most powerful of these patterns is the process by which two people are initially drawn together, which I have come to refer to as **The Invisible Connection**. Traditional issues—such as having common interests, finding a person physically attractive, charming, intelligent, funny, and otherwise appealing—**do** matter very much, but not quite in the way that we usually think. Traits such as these provide the basis upon which we *like* someone, or *enjoy* them, or *get along with* them, or feel *affection* toward them, but they are not necessarily the **primary** reason we choose them as a partner. We choose our boyfriends, girlfriends, husbands, and wives for certain reasons that we are largely unaware of. In fact, even the word "choice" is in some ways an inaccurate term to use when it comes to relationships.

Learning to Know the Unknown

At the core of every couple is the "magnet" that drew them together in the first place, which is the Invisible Connection. There are two essential "secrets" that control this process. First, you must understand what's meant by the term "unconscious." Most people have heard this term before and have a general understanding of its meaning. This information is definitely not intended to sound "shrinky," but since so much of what influences our relationships is hidden, in order to fully and accurately understand them, you must also fully and accurately understand the term "unconscious."

If you consider human functioning as a whole—thoughts, feelings, reactions, choices—you can basically split it into two approximately equal parts: 50 percent conscious and 50 percent unconscious. "Conscious" refers to those things that we are fully aware of, that we can put it into words and describe. "Unconscious" literally means "not conscious," and the amount of awareness that we have of these parts of ourselves is none. Zero. Zilch. This tends to be a rather uncomfortable concept for most people (including me) to digest. If we truly get it, it means that there are major aspects of our lives (choices, reactions) about which we have *absolutely no awareness whatsoever*. This is often not a very pleasant thought for most of us; after all, our whole existence as human beings is typically built around the concept of controlling our own destiny.

To make matters worse, **we're not even aware that we're not aware**. Almost never will you find that a person has no reason for their behavior, feelings, or choices. In fact, we essentially *always* have some conscious explanation for the things that we do, and, what's more, those reasons usually make sense; they tend to be reasonable, believable. Unfortunately, this system creates what amounts to a "booby trap" built into human nature. About half the time, the explanation that we may give is correct; the reason we think we've done what we've done is *actually* the reason. However, the other half of the time we give just as believable an explanation, except that it has nothing to do with the truth; the real reason is one that we are just not aware of (because it's unconscious). This is the booby trap; how are we supposed to tell the difference?

The fact is, we usually can't, because whether conscious or unconscious, the explanations have the same appearance on the surface. For example, take two women who are twins. They're now grown women, thirty-five years of age, normal, etc. I ask one of them if it bothered her growing up as a twin; she thinks about it for a moment, and then says, "Well, I love my sister, but, yeah, there were a few things that were tough growing up. You know, we were compared a lot, and sometimes people thought I'd feel the same as her even though I was a separate person . . . stuff like that."

Now that is probably a fully accurate answer, as opposed to the other woman's response to the same question: (thinks for a moment) "No, not at all. My sister's my best friend in the world, and I have no complaints whatsoever." In this case, I wouldn't believe her, but not because I think she's lying. The problem is that the conscious and unconscious are essentially two completely **separate zones**. For simplicity's sake, let's say that the conscious is in your head, and the unconscious is in your belly. So, when the women answers the question, she searches the only part she can (her head) for any evidence that says she's "mad at her sister." Because there really isn't any there, she concludes that there isn't any **at all**. However, what if the part that says "I'm mad at my sister" is contained in her belly? No matter how long she looks, she won't (and can't) find it, because that information is simply not contained *in the zone she's looking in.*

To clarify it a bit further, ask yourself this question: what *type* of information tends to get stored in the unconscious? That's right . . . thoughts, feelings, and experiences that are often painful or unpleasant. In fact, the brain is actually *motivated* to hide this type of uncomfortable, yet highly influential information. Because so many relevant parts of ourselves end up being hidden, it's difficult for us to ever be totally sure of our perceptions. Therefore, if we were going to be more accurate in our use of language, whenever we were giving an explanation for our actions or feelings, we would have to say something like, "Well, as far as I'm *aware of*, this is why I did that, but then again, there could be something else going on that I don't see." What a pain. You can tell why people generally avoid their unconscious; things can get "messier" when you begin trying to understand yourself on a deeper level. You may discover a lot of valuable information, but it can also be confusing and, at times, painful.

It should be noted that this definition of the unconscious is a working, practical one, not necessarily a literal one. There's no way to absolutely determine exactly how much of a particular person's life is being unconsciously or consciously controlled. In addition, we have a third part of our experience, referred to as "subconscious," which means that we're *partially* aware of something. So, it's not so important to know precisely how much of you is acting unconsciously, as much as it is to recognize the overall reality that much of what we as human beings do is based on things we may not be fully aware of, nor able to fully control.

By the way, it should not be concluded that there's something wrong with someone if they have a lot of unconscious stuff going on inside them. If that were true, then it would have to be true for all of us. It's part of the human condition, and if you're alive, then you've got a major portion of you that's hidden. Not only is this normal, it's *healthy*. The human brain controls a number of extremely important survival functions, and one of them is to protect us from information that could do us harm.

Because the information contained in the unconscious is hidden, it is of course difficult to know what's really "in there." This dilemma is further complicated by the fact that the unconscious cannot be viewed *directly*; it can't be precisely located or measured. Therefore, the only tools that we have to determine its contents are indirect ones. Fortunately, human beings have a way of providing evidence of their unconscious through their behavior. Nonetheless, we're still only able to see correlations, to deduce the triggers that are going on underneath from observable behaviors on the surface. Although the best we can do is to gather "circumstantial evidence," human nature reliably provides us with plenty of it, due to the fact that **all people are consistent in their core personality traits and corresponding actions**. Thus, the key to uncovering the unconscious is not found in individual behaviors as it is in **patterns** of behavior. This could be summarized as follows: see the *pattern*, see the *person*.

One client, who was particularly wedded to the concept of logic and observable facts, found the whole idea of the unconscious to be fluffy and unscientific. Her philosophy was basically, "If it can't be seen, it doesn't exist." However, when asked why certain types of situations bother *her*, she stated, "It's just the way I am." As you can see, that in itself is not a very scientific explanation. One of the most solid rules of human behavior you can find is this: when it comes to things that people do **consistently**, no one does anything "just because." If it's a pattern, it's being done for some clearly identifiable, systematic reason. The fact that the reason may not be immediately obvious is a separate issue.

Since there is always a cause underneath these types of behaviors, the (probable) cause can nearly always be identified. In this woman's case, although she came from a loving family, her parents tended to get overly worked up about everyday situations, which to her seemed highly irrational. As a result, she gradually developed her intense need for things to make sense, to be based on reliable evidence. So, the "secret" to understanding the unconscious is to know what to look for; to find the clues, the trail of bread crumbs, that human beings inevitably leave behind. These tools will be examined in more detail as the book proceeds.

A Paradox of Human Development—That Which Shapes Us the Most We Remember the Least

Because most adults don't remember much of anything before the age of five or six (other than a few scattered incidents), we tend to think of that period of our lives as mostly insignificant, kind of like we were just "blobs." However, all you have to do is spend a couple of hours with a three year old, and you see just how much they're anything *but* blobs. If they want to do something, and you say "no," do they just say, "Oh, okay," and then sit quietly? No way! Typically, you'll know when they're dissatisfied, and probably so will your eardrums. They have their own independent thoughts, feelings, and opinions. I could give literally millions of examples to show just how *aware* children are, and how much they *care* about what's going on around them (especially things that involve their family), but here's one. A parent told me that their four-year-old child made a comment, on their own, asking another family member, "Is Grandpa going to have a beer?" Where did that question, and all of the thought (and feelings) behind it come from? Such is the amazing observational skills and insight of a child at work. If you've spent any time around young kids, you know that they don't miss a thing.

So, if Daddy promised to be home at 6:30 to watch a special TV program with his three-year-old daughter, you can just picture her sitting by the window watching for his car and waiting for him. By 7 p.m., if he's not home, you'd probably find a little girl still sitting there with tears on her face. Did Dad do this to be hurtful? Not at all. Does it mean he doesn't care about and love his daughter with all his heart? No, he's just not perfect. But, to the daughter, it still *hurts*. Because the child's brain functions differently than the adult brain, children (at least to the age of six) have what's called an "ego-centric" point of view. That's not meant to be an insult; they literally see things from the perspective of themselves as the center of the universe. This is why young kids will often ask, "Why is the moon following us?" They know there's only one moon, and that there are other cars besides the one that they're in, yet the one moon is following *them*. Because of this phenomenon, children tend to blame anything bad or upsetting that happens in their household on themselves. Even though it may not be at all their fault (e.g., parents fighting or divorce), they'll assume that it is. It's just the way that their brain works at that age.

For example, an associate of mine told me a story that typifies a child's tendency to personalize everything, especially upsetting events. While leaving for work one day, this person slipped while walking to her car. It so happened that her five-year-old child was watching and waving good-bye at the time. Well, the mother ended up breaking her leg, which was of course very unfortunate, but had absolutely nothing to do with the child's actions. Regardless, the child was hysterical, in tears, largely due to his belief that he was somehow responsible for his Mom's accident. Talk about a no-win situation—despite all of the reassurances in the world from his parents, the child will still inevitably internalize some of this guilt...regardless of the fact that it's no one's fault. This truly is not a "good" or a "bad" thing, but rather just an inescapable part of the process of growing up.

So, in its role of protecting us from too many of these painful feelings, the unconscious is crucial to our survival. The previously mentioned little girl who was waiting to watch T.V. with Daddy will feel hurt and, at least to some degree, angry toward him for not keeping his promise. On the other hand, kids at this age genuinely worship both of their parents, and they certainly wouldn't want to feel angry toward either one of them. As we all know, having conflicting (both positive and negative) feelings toward someone as an adult is uncomfortable enough, but it's even tougher for a child, especially if it's about their parents. So, the brain protects them, storing the unpleasant feelings underneath, thus getting rid of the conflict. The little girl is once again free to adore her Daddy. This is very functional, because it allows her to concentrate on the childhood tasks that she needs to address, such as reading, writing, manners, and getting along with other kids. However, *where did all of that stored information go*? More on that later.

The Hidden Attraction in Relationships

Now for the two essential, and little-known, relationship "secrets." The first is that the selection of a partner is largely controlled by the **unconscious**. This flies in the face of the conventional assumption that it's a *choice* based entirely on the person having a combination of features that we find highly desirable. The second (and maybe even more disturbing) dynamic is that the unconscious is specifically motivated to select a partner mainly for *dysfunctional* reasons. As odd as that may initially sound, the more you think about it, the more sense it will begin to make. For instance, it provides clear answers to some seemingly unanswerable questions, such as why people often seem to keep having the same relationship or the same arguments over and over, despite their best efforts to the contrary.

I realize that the word "dysfunctional" is a loaded term, but its use is not intended to be taken in a pejorative manner, but literally, as in a system that has some inherent flaw built into it that will tend to produce a breakdown of that system. Many people may think of the term dysfunctional as implying a generally "neurotic" person, but that's not necessarily true (it may or may not be, but of course, all people are neurotic in their own way). In this case, it refers to the fact that we as human beings have an amazingly accurate "radar" to find people who are dysfunctional in ways with which we have had much previous experience, e.g., in ways that resemble our **parents**. You know that old expression, "You marry your mother/father?" Well, guess what? Unfortunately, it's not just a cliché. Although we've all heard it, we may not have truly understood (or wanted to understand) its meaning, and so most people end up just disregarding it. But when we as a society have a divorce rate that hovers around fifty percent, it's hard to escape the fact that the commonly accepted rules and information that we use to guide our relationships do not work particularly well.

When people initially hear the concept of the Invisible Connection, they have basically two types of reactions. Sometimes the connection is obvious to them; they grew up with a critical parent, and it's clear, now that the issue's been raised, that their partner is critical as well. Often, however, the connection isn't obvious, and the person says, "My husband/wife/boyfriend/girlfriend is nothing like my parents!" Many times people are unable to recognize the connection because they focus on specific personality traits or behaviors, rather than on the theme, or the *essence*, of those traits or behaviors. It's the overall **principle** that's involved, not the details.

For example, let's say a woman grew up with a father who's an alcoholic. He worked, and he wasn't at all abusive, and he was caring, but he drank too much. At first, she would deny any similarity between her father and her husband. Given that she was well aware that her father's alcoholism was a source of pain for her, she had clearly determined in her own mind that she would never marry a man who was an alcohol abuser. She knew that this was the last thing she would want in her marriage. So, she proclaims, "See, this theory doesn't apply to me...my husband doesn't drink at all!"

However, the key issue of the child who grows up with the alcoholic parent is not the alcohol consumption itself, but rather the effect that it has on the *relationship* with the child. A common consequence of the drinking is that is creates a lack of **availability** of that parent; he is either actually out of the house drinking, or, even when he is home, he's often not really available, because he's intoxicated. He's kind of "there but not there." Ironically, children whose fathers were surgeons will have basically the same issue, which may at first seem puzzling, because the surgeon is saving people's lives, doing something that society greatly respects, whereas that may not apply to the alcoholic father. However, despite the best intentions, they're still both largely unavailable to their children.

This is the real issue, the *principle* that is involved. Even though the woman in the above example found a husband who doesn't drink at all, she still ends up with the same basic behavior *pattern*. It turns out that she married someone who (fill in the blank): works sixty-five hours a week and is rarely home, or someone who's a sports fanatic and is usually involved in some type of sports-related activity, or someone who's unable to have an intimate conversation because he's usually on the computer or watching TV; in other words, someone who's also largely *unavailable*, like her father. Oops.

The good news is, when it comes to looking for, or trying to maintain, a truly loving relationship, we're all in the same boat. In fact, there are many ways in which our society at least partly recognizes the phenomenon of the Invisible Connection. For instance, many popular clichés refer to aspects of the pattern:

"love is blind"; "opposites attract"; "women always seem to go for 'bad boys'"; "you marry your mother/father"; "there's a thin line between love and hate"; "can't live with 'em, can't live without 'em"; "we always hurt the ones we love." Although not well explained, these common expressions do indicate our basic, intuitive awareness that relationships contain an inherent tension, a struggle, a push-pull dynamic that, at least to some degree, is unavoidable.

Emotional Bruises: A Normal Part of Growing Up

The essential feature of the Invisible Connection is that the unconscious has an uncanny ability to find potential partners who have fundamental similarities to our parents, especially those characteristics that we experienced as painful, frustrating, upsetting, disappointing, or otherwise undesirable. These characteristics tend to revolve around major themes, as opposed to specific details. There are only so many of these principles available, and therefore at least two or three of them will apply to any given person. I call these "Jars" (which will be further explained later), and they are:

1. (lack of) attention
2. (lack of) affection
3. (lack of) expression
4. fear/anger
5. loss/abandonment
6. physical neglect
7. fairness
8. respect
9. inconsideration/self-centeredness
10. dependability
11. control
12. irrationality/inconsistency
13. ambivalence/passivity
14. trust/loyalty
15. availability
16. criticism/perfectionism/self-esteem
17. guilt/obligation/responsibility
18. closed-mindedness/rigidity

These dynamics are, at least to some degree, a universal part of the human experience, but they have a particularly significant impact on the psychological and emotional development of a child. If we exclude the relatively small segment of the parenting population who are actually abusive in some way, the remaining portion is made up of basically good, well-meaning parents; those who care greatly about their children and would never do anything intentionally to harm them. Unfortunately, **parenting is literally an impossible job**. All parents are human, and as such, have issues of their own. These issues tend to leak out in parent's behavior, albeit unintentionally. It is unavoidable that some of this "baggage" ends up being incorporated into a child's makeup, and it's what provides the basis for the "Invisible Connection," the traits that we unconsciously, systematically find in our partners.

Childhood Issues—The Blueprint for Adult Relationships

Given that these parts of our relationship with our parents were basically unpleasant, it begs the question: why in the world would we want to find a partner who will repeat the same unpleasant behaviors? Didn't we have enough of them while we were growing up? It might not seem to make sense, except for the concept of **mastery**. We as human beings are born with a powerful, never-ending need to create positive outcomes in our experiences, to successfully complete tasks.

For example, a common game for a six-month-old child is to throw an object out of their crib, and wait for an adult to retrieve it. Give it back to them, and what's the first thing that they do? Throw it back out again. The profound look of glee that appears on the child's face is the feeling of mastery ("I did it!"). This is the six-month-old version of mastery, but the need never stops, we just continue finding more advanced ways to accomplish it. Potty training, eating with a knife and fork, and learning the ABCs are all examples of a child's constant need for achievement and overcoming challenges. Another (simple) example? Video games. Mess up, and what's the first thing most people do? Hit "reset" ("There's no way this stupid game is gonna get the better of *me*"). As children grow, they take on the tasks involved in education, sports, and other hobbies. Throughout adulthood, we continue on this path, endeavoring to conquer careers and finances.

This need to create positive outcomes extends into all areas of life, and is with us until the day that we die. For a child, however, there is no more important place for this to occur than in the relationship with his/her parents. However, there's a major obstacle in the way of this particular area of mastery—the child ultimately has no power, no control, over his or her circumstances. Therefore, there's little or no opportunity for mastery where the child/parent relationship is concerned. The parents call the shots, for good or for bad, and children have no choice but to live with them. Although in the majority of families the overall experience for a child is mostly positive, there are virtually always a few (typically two or three) what we can call "issues." These are things that the child has experienced as unpleasant on a consistent basis growing up. These areas of psychological and emotional "sensitivity" are not the result of abuse, but rather the natural consequence of the inevitable conflicts that arise over the years between parents and children, as well as the parent's own issues.

For instance, many loving, well-meaning parents are also somewhat perfectionistic; things need to be neat or done in a particular way. This is a very common trait among successful people (in fact, I've come to call this "successful person's disease"). In many ways, these traits are highly desirable and help to foster achievement. Naturally, children may adopt some of these successful habits from their parents. Children are so connected to their parents that they will automatically absorb some of their issues, just due to frequent exposure. For instance, I know one girl who, when she was three, walked into the bathroom (after I had just used it) and indignantly stated, "You got water all over the sink!"

Mind you, her parents were not the type to be controlling and always telling their children to clean things up. However, they themselves were both quite neat, and tended to keep their home in an orderly fashion. Without them intentionally doing anything to subject their daughter to this standard of behavior, she picked it up on her own, like a sponge. Is this irrelevant (i.e., will it have no meaningful impact on this girl's life)? To the contrary. At age nine, she still had the same tendency for order, and was in fact aware of it, commenting, "It just makes me, kind of, you know, like in a bad mood, if things aren't where they're supposed to be." This is neither good nor bad; it just reveals how much children really *are* being impacted by their environment.

It also raises another important issue, which is that so much of human behavior could be described as a "double-edged sword." This little girl had developed a very good work ethic that can serve her well in many future endeavors. On the other side of the same coin there are often some undesirable effects as well, some emotional "bruising." When the parent says, "Don't do it that way, do it this way," they may in fact be helping the child to develop more effective skills, but to the child it also "stings" a little.

By itself, this one incident would basically be irrelevant, and would have no substantive impact on the child's development. However, these behaviors tend to be part of a pattern; they usually happen *consistently* over an extended period of time. Just imagine—eighteen years of life, multiplied by 365 days in a year—that's a lot of opportunities for these little nicks and bruises to occur. In fact, in its first six years of life, a child is awake for approximately *20,000 hours*. When the nicks occur in the same location hundreds or even thousands of times, they gradually become a **wound**. As stated earlier, we all have at least two or three of these sensitive spots, and wherever they are, we are extremely prone to overreacting when they're poked.

Childhood Issues (Wounds) and Everyday Life (Salt)

There are few absolute rules in life, but one that comes very close is this: whenever you notice anyone getting hot and bothered about any situation (excluding obvious traumatic events like violent crime, sudden loss of a loved one, etc.), it is a dead giveaway that one of their childhood issues has been activated. When someone quickly reacts with irritation, anger, or a sense of urgency, they are almost always **unconsciously** reacting to an issue with which they have had much previous negative experience. The reaction is unconscious because the individual is almost never aware that a childhood button has been pushed. We are all extremely prone to this type of overreaction, and it provides the basis for most day-to-day conflicts among friends, coworkers, and lovers. A crucial point to this pattern is that we are not *aware* that there are really two issues going on: one about whatever just happened, and the other about the pre-existing issue, or **Jar**. The Jars provide the blueprint for the things that we'll overreact to throughout our lives.

If I had a dollar for every time a couple made the statement, "but we rarely fight about anything important—it's always little stuff!" I would be a multimillionaire. So it's not that these overreactions of ours are insignificant. In fact, they're the basis for

17

what is actually one of the most important reasons for the couple being together in the first place; they are the "Invisible Connection." Along with all the wonderful, traditional benefits that come with being involved with someone, there is this extremely unromantic, yet crucial function; to give ourselves the opportunity to fight and win previously unresolved conflicts with our parents (in effect, providing ourselves with an ongoing series of "second chances").

Mastery—The Hidden Agenda in Relationships

Underneath the formation of every longterm romantic relationship is the issue of **mastery**. There's no more important place for us to gain this than with our parents, but because, as previously mentioned, we don't possess the necessary control to establish it as children, mastery is never achieved. We grow up, we move out of our parents' homes, and we begin to make our way into adulthood. Yet there's something missing; there's still a huge "unmastered" area that remains from childhood. So, the unconscious has a very specific agenda; it essentially says, "Well, if I can't go back and master these issues with my *actual* parents, the **next best** place to do it would be...with my partner."

Because the principles we fight about with our partners are the ones that were never overcome with our parents, the feelings run very deep and strong, and therefore cause deep and strong reactions. Although the battle is mostly really with our parent (or parents), we fight with our partner, because he or she is the one who's available. If we win against our partner, then we are **retroactively, symbolically winning against our parents**, and that is why we fight so hard to win. From the unconscious standpoint, there's a deep-down belief that by getting the *final* victory, we'll be able to wipe away all previous losses. This dynamic largely explains why people often have a strong positive reaction when they know that someone has cleared a hurdle after many previous failures. For example, many people (whether sports fans or not) were happy to see John Elway finally win a Super Bowl in 1998—he "instantly" went from being the ultimate loser to the ultimate winner; he overcame adversity and triumphed in the end. We as human beings crave mastery and are driven by that need in almost everything we do.

Unintentionally Finding a Partner
Who Will Open Up Your Jars

It's important to remember that this is an **automatic, unconscious** process. The two or three issues that we struggled with our parents about were difficult enough to deal with in childhood. Even though most people continue to love and respect their parents, they also know we didn't like those particular issues at the time. Why the heck would we want to find them in a spouse or significant other? On the surface, we wouldn't; the conscious brain is looking for characteristics that are appealing and enjoyable, that we find value in (common interests, sense of humor, attractiveness, intelligence, etc.). These are the qualities that we are typically *aware* of looking for in a partner, the ones that we learn from society.

However, in humans, there are always two levels of functioning going on simultaneously. Practically speaking, we live in what amounts to **"dual realities,"** one based on the conscious, or *visible*, the other on the unconscious, or *invisible*. While the conscious is seeking the most positive traits in an individual, the unconscious has its own agenda: **find someone who will most effectively re-create the worst aspects of your parents, in order to give you multiple**

opportunities to grapple with those issues and master them.

I'm not happy to report this; I realize it's a rather unromantic view of relationships; it isn't *sexy*. However, I can't avoid reporting it, because I (and many other clinicians) have found the clinical evidence for this pattern to be overwhelming. For example, in the past several years of practice, I've worked with well over a thousand clients who are representative of everyday, "normal" people. Whether they're professionals, laborers, or unemployed, old or young, educated or not, they all have one thing in common; they all have their own version of the Invisible Connection. This holds true not only for those people I know professionally, but personally as well, including many with happy, successful relationships.

The Hidden Marriage Vow

It is somewhat humorous that, hidden underneath all of the traditional marriage vows, there's the "hidden marriage vow": "Do you take _____ to be your lawfully wedded spouse, to love, honor, and cherish, and willingly volunteer to be the receptacle for all of their stored-up childhood pain and frustration?" On second thought, maybe it's better to leave that one out.

Relationships truly are a major part of the joy and beauty of life, so this is not to suggest that we find our partners due *only* to dysfunctional reasons; much of what draws and keeps people together are the healthy things that we love and appreciate about them, their unique and attractive qualities. However, if you were to slice up a "relationship pie," as many positive pieces as there may be, **none will be bigger than the Invisible Connection**.

One additional characteristic of this pattern is that there's a fascinating, almost unbelievable accuracy in the way that two people will fit together psychologically. It's been my experience to observe in hundreds of couples that people who are polar opposites in a *very crucial area* will find each other. A very insecure and jealous person and a highly flirtatious person end up together. A person with an intense need for organization will marry a highly disorganized person. Note that if the jealous person were with the disorganized person, there would be no problem; those sensitivities don't match up; they won't create any particular friction. However, the systematic nature of the Invisible Connection is that one partner's dysfunction will irritate the other's *in the most effective manner possible*; in other words, in the most frustrating possible way! This nearly perfect "dysfunctional symmetry" is the core of the Invisible Connection, and indicates just how accurate the "radar" of the unconscious can be.

The connection is so specific that it can be thought of as essentially a "hinge" that ties the whole relationship together. The exact nature of each couple's Invisible Connection is nearly always this: the partners will both have an "injury," or Jar, in the same emotional area (e.g., self-esteem, trust, respect, etc.). They will therefore share a common *pain*—for instance, both may feel insecure about their desirability to others. This obviously would be something that would have drawn them together in the first place, the feeling of being *understood* by each other, of having a common bond. Unfortunately, however pleasing this sense of kinship is, it is also the very point at which the couple experiences their greatest frustration with one another. They find common ground in the pain that they brought *to* the relationship, but their paths go in different directions when it comes to the **method of coping** with that pain (also referred to as "defenses").

This produces a specific incompatibility that's unique to that particular couple, a combustibility, a...chemistry. The jealous person's comfort (of their self-esteem Jar) comes from being totally monogamous, whereas the flirtatious person's comes from getting constant positive feedback from others. They are both acceptable coping mechanisms, *but not with each other*. Ironically, this is one of the essential ingredients that pulled them together in the first place.

A common (and sadly ironic) outcome of this pattern is that: **something that you want and need from your partner the most is the very thing that they give you the least**. For example, one couple that I worked with had this "yin/yang" dynamic around dependability and guilt. His Jar was dependability; although he loved his mother greatly and knew she loved him, she was often unreliable when he was growing up, and would frequently not follow through on commitments. Her Jar was guilt; although she loved her father greatly and knew he loved her, he tended to make her feel guilty growing up, at times with direct "guilt trips," and at others through indirect implication. These issues were areas of sensitivity for each of them, areas in which they had suffered many previous "losses."

Her unreliable behavior kept opening up his dependability Jar, while his hurt and angry reaction, which implied she had done something wrong, kept opening up her guilt Jar. Her sensitivity to guilt often tended to make her avoid confrontation, which would then lead her to not follow through on a commitment. When she would communicate a change in plans directly, his sensitivity to unreliability would cause him to overreact and make her feel guilty, thus encouraging her to avoid future direct communications. This is what's referred to as a "vicious cycle." While they were very much in love, and in fact enjoyed each other's company tremendously, this pattern caused them consistent pain and frustration, and threatened the stability of their relationship.

Seeing Beyond the Details of Conflict—
It's the Principle That Counts

Given these patterns, it's no surprise that couples tend to argue about whatever their Invisible Connection issues are. In fact, couples will essentially have the same two or three arguments over and over. The details and the dates may change, but the core issues of the conflicts remain the same (violations of trust, battles for control, matters of consideration, etc.). Even when couples fight very infrequently, you find that when they *do* fight, they tend to fight about their Invisible Connection(s). As mentioned previously, the types of issues that make up the pattern are large, thematic issues, or *principles*. It's fascinating to discover how many everyday events actually boil down to these core issues, or **Jars**. Details and situations that appear to have absolutely nothing to do with these deeper concepts on the surface turn out to be, upon closer inspection, principles "dressed up" as details.

For example, I once had an experience with a partner in which I had asked her to pick me up some donuts after work. When I got home the next day, I saw the donut bag on the fridge. Excited, I went in to thank her and proceeded to remove the donuts from the bag. As I looked with anticipation, I began pulling out two types of donuts: one which I had asked for, and one that I hadn't (a poofy chocolate iced donut). I said to her, "What are these?!" She replied, "Chocolate glazed donuts, just what you asked for." Aware that she definitely knew the difference, I immediately replied, "No I *didn't*. I asked for chocolate *cake* donuts!" She obviously was not too happy with this response.

As I retreated to the kitchen, I noticed that I was very angry, and felt a strong need to go into the other room and pick a fight with her. Now, given that I discuss with clients on a daily basis the pattern that overreactions are a dead giveaway that a childhood issue has been activated, I was feeling somewhat puzzled. What important principle could she have violated? You may have surmised by now that I probably never had any traumatic childhood donut experiences. Therefore, the more reasonable part of my brain told me that there must be *something else* going on. The question was, what? What could my childhood possibly have to do with getting the wrong kind of donuts? And then it hit me...all I had to do was think of the **principle** involved, then ask myself if that was an issue that was familiar from my childhood. Ah-ha...this was an issue of *irrationality*, about someone using a thought process that doesn't make *sense*. This issue (unlike donuts) **is** important enough to fight about.

It's interesting to note that this realization did not really take away my intense desire to pick the fight with my partner. My impulses kept pulling at me, wanting me to go into the other room and tell her, for the record, that she was wrong. This clarifies an important aspect of the Invisible Connection; that the unconscious is highly motivated to pin the blame on your partner. Previously, when discussing the function of the unconscious to store away unpleasant feelings in order to protect us as children, the question was posed, "What happens to the feelings?" Well, when it comes to human beings, there are only two options: the energy is either **processed** or **stored**. Unfortunately, the third (and much more popular) answer, which is "Leave them alone and they'll just go away" is **not** an available option. The human animal is simply not constructed that way, despite the fact that many people (myself included) may prefer it if we were. Thus, despite the natural tendency for us to *want* to avoid dealing with unpleasant issues and feelings, it ultimately doesn't really work—because the reality is, those issues and feelings still *exist*.

Processed or stored, what does that mean? Psychologically, we "process" thoughts, feelings, and experiences by engaging in some type of activity that provides a means of expression, of working, of manipulating. Processing takes something from one state or form and changes it into another. Dough is dough—it's still made of flour, shortening, water, etc.—but it's the kneading *process* that transforms it into a useable product. Sure, massages feel good, but there's a *process* of pressure and manipulation that literally alters muscular tension. These and many other examples have a crucial element in common; none of them primarily occur *automatically*. There is a consciousness, a purposefulness, an *effort* that must be made in order for them to happen. This is the fundamental ingredient necessary for psychological and emotional processing. Exactly *how* a given person chooses to achieve this result is largely up to them and their own emotional and intellectual "style." Typical methods include: **emotional** expression (crying and feeling), **verbal/cognitive** expression (talking, thinking, and writing), and **physical** expression (safe forms of aggression, such as working out or breaking a specifically designated object).

While all people engage in this process to some degree as a natural part of everyday functioning, the system is highly imperfect. Because we have such an incredible *volume* of experiences, there's a built-in tendency for us to have more "coming in" than "going out." In an ideal system, every experience that we have (each of which creates a certain amount of, for lack of a better term, emotional/psychological "energy") would be **processed fully at the time of the experience**. However, as healthy as this might be emotionally, it would be highly impractical, and therefore *unhealthy* with respect to one's ability to *function*. Talk about a paradox...in order to function effectively, we must avoid dealing with a certain amount of our emotional energy, but then that energy gets stored and comes back to haunt us. This is what I mean when I say that there are booby traps built into human nature.

To make the situation even more complicated, since the energy being stored is consistently greater than the energy being processed, it creates an ongoing system of **buildup**. What do you think would happen if you continued to pump energy into a confined space? All Monty Python images aside, human beings don't usually actually explode. Assuming someone doesn't have a literal "breakdown" (which can in fact be the result of this type of buildup), the energy has to go *somewhere*. For healthy, normal people, the most common result is that it basically "leaks" out. Imagine a container whose walls are fairly strong and stable, but which also has a few select weak points. When the pressure reaches a sufficient level, the weak points provide openings, or **outlets**. As you may have guessed, these vulnerable spots are those areas that have been gradually nicked and bruised over time—they are the Jars.

As mentioned, it would be extremely maladaptive for us to have to process every bit of emotional energy that got created throughout our lives. This would essentially mean that we would have to spend an equal amount of time reflecting on our experiences as we would living them; you can see how impractical that would be, because it simply wouldn't allow us enough time to then take care of the business of *living*. Thus, life presents us with another double-edged sword; where do we draw the line? What is the proper balance between processing and functioning? This will be explored more thoroughly in the final chapter.

Your Personal Arsenal of Stored-up Energy

For our purposes at this point, though, there's still the dilemma created by the built-up, stored energy compressed into the finite container. If the weak points are the Jars, and outlets are created for the pressurized energy to escape, then situations provide us with the *opportunity* to vent some of that energy. Notice I use the word "opportunity," which implies an active, *motivated* process. Given that we all have this unavoidable reservoir of accumulated feelings, and given that it's made up of mostly unpleasant, painful feelings, and that it's filling up a confined space and pushing out on the walls, it should be no surprise that the result is an *uncomfortable state*. Since we are biologically programmed to relieve such states of tension, it is natural for us to seek an outlet, a way of *discharging* this energy.

The product of this process is what I call **heat-seeking missiles**. These are the stored-up feelings "looking" for opportunities to be released. Fortunately, life provides us with infinite chances to launch heat-seeking missiles. Unfortunately, people, and particularly those we love, tend to be the targets. Actual heat-seeking missiles actively pursue their targets, and cause damage when they make impact; this is also the case for human ones. However, unlike actual missiles, the human version's primary purpose is not necessarily to do harm—it's often more of an undesirable side-effect that they may injure those we know and/or love. There are two main objectives of the human heat-seeking missile: (1) to provide **relief** of stored-up, pressurized feelings/energy, and (2) to offer invaluable opportunities for **mastery** of previously unmastered experiences (yes, there's that mastery thing again).

If you gain only one thing from this discussion, hopefully it will be that this is not a process that's passive, nor random, but rather is one that is **highly motivated and systematic**.

However, it's also vitally important to note that the person is not necessarily launching heat-seeking missiles *on purpose*, at least not consciously. This particular system is truly guided by the unconscious parts of our brain. Loosely put, it knows exactly what it's doing and what its agenda is, but the *person* may not. Although the system that controls this process is typically "invisible," the *results* of the process are highly visible. When you or your partner say something mean, or angry, or critical, or hurtful, it will be quite clear to one or both of you.

Learning to stop launching these missiles at your partner is not an easy thing to do. For one thing, at least initially, it is a **fully automatic process**. Secondly, as previously discussed, this process of mastery (which at times can closely resemble payback or revenge) is one of the main reasons why you and your partner chose each other to begin with! The ways to begin to be more aware of this system, and the tools that can be used to gain more control over it, will be discussed in the final chapter.

Meanwhile, in most couples' everyday life, heated arguments or breakdowns in communication tend to begin over something "stupid." Even though the true fuel for the missile that's just been launched came from many years ago, the fresh *spark* that ignited that fuel came from just now, with your partner, and *he/she is the one that's in the room*. What a perfect opportunity! Even though the real battle underneath may be with your parents, you get the chance to act it out on an actual person (your partner) right here, right now.

Besides, we *want* the partner to be the bad guy, because if the negative feelings aren't about them, then they must be about our *parents*. This is unacceptable. We tend to be biologically programmed (for good reason) to see our parents in a positive light, and it is generally uncomfortable for us to see our parents' faults. Even for those who *consciously* have a more complete understanding of their parents' strengths and weaknesses, the *unconscious* has an agenda to maintain its childlike image of the perfect parent. As a result, even though our feelings are largely about our parents, it is still the partner who we take it out on. Understandably, the partner is usually not thrilled with this arrangement, and they have their own reaction to the other person's reaction...sound familiar? This is actually how most arguments are started, and then it just escalates; another example of that "vicious cycle."

The push and pull of these core issues in a relationship is extremely frustrating for those involved. We tend to maintain a vitally important interpretation in our own heads about the other person's behavior, something to the effect of: "I don't understand why he/she can't *get this*. I've told him/her that this is important to me over and over, yet he/she still *refuses* to honor my wishes!" This is the need for mastery in action, the attempt to symbolically win the battles with the parents that were never won in childhood.

Dysfunctional Glue

Another crucial dimension of this pattern is the fact that the Jars tend to be hidden to begin with (thus the name *Invisible* Connection). Time after time, couples will sit in my office and tell me, "But I didn't *know* that he/she had these behaviors! They didn't really start happening until (two years into the relationship, three years after we got married, the past year or so, etc)." Almost invariably, the very next words out of the person's mouth are something like, "Except, well, there was that one time when...," and then they go on to tell a story about a situation in which their partner displayed the very same behavior that has now brought them into therapy together. In fact, it turns out that this (now unacceptable behavior) is almost always revealed very early on in the relationship, typically within the first three dates.

For example, one woman was aware that she had an unavailability Jar (due to her father being extremely emotionally unavailable throughout her childhood). She was well aware that she did not like this trait, and that she longed for a partner who would be fully present and attentive. After two weeks or so of dating, she presented this new relationship in therapy. She reported how wonderful he was, how sweet, caring, etc. I inquired if there might be any ways in which she'd noticed that he had any of her father's (or parents') less desirable qualities. She thought about it and responded, "Well, the only thing is that we've known each other for two weeks, but I've only seen him three times" (due to his job). She then went on to say, "But I don't really think that's going to be a problem, because he won't always be working this particular schedule."

I cannot tell you how revealing those twelve words are (*"but I don't really think that's going to be a problem, because..."*). In my experience, that phrase is one of the most telling and reliable predictors of what eventually turns out to be the central area of complaint and/or conflict for the couple. It could be thought of as the "dysfunctional glue" of the relationship, and it appears to be present in all romantic partnerships.

Having said that, it is important to point out that this dysfunctional glue is *relative*; it's not uniform for all couples. Relationships, like so many things, can be viewed on a continuum, from (for lack of better terms) "least dysfunctional" to "most dysfunctional." Most of us probably know at least one couple in each of these more extreme categories. The "least dysfunctional" is the type of relationship that most of us aspire to; people who are happy that they're with each other, get along well overall, and find their time together to be much more satisfying than not.

Even within this "healthy" type of relationship, there are still problems to deal with. It's probably not surprising to you that there's no such thing as the ideal relationship; all couples have some level of conflict and friction. As mentioned before, *everyone* has their issues, their "quirks." Since there are no completely psychologically "healthy" people, there cannot be completely healthy couples. When it comes to human beings, there are basically three types of relationships: good/great with problems, pretty good with problems, or bad with problems. If you talk with actual couples, you'll find that you never get the answer, "Our relationship has no problems whatsoever."

So, whether you're fortunate enough to be in one of the genuinely constructive relationships, unfortunate enough to be in one of the genuinely destructive ones, or somewhere in between, you will still have *your own version* of the dysfunctional glue. You may have fights or disagreements; they may be quiet or loud, long or short, aggressive or passive. You and your partner may get on each other's nerves, say hurtful things, quietly grumble at each other, or yell at the top of your lungs. Your arguments may happen ten times a year, ten times a month, or ten times a day. Nonetheless, if you look closely enough at the **pattern** of those conflicts and the **principles** involved, you'll see your dysfunctional glue, your Invisible Connection. While there are an infinite number of specific situations that can cause a potential argument between partners, they all boil down to only a few principles, or Jars.

The practical benefit of understanding this concept is that you end up only having to deal with six or so issues—a much more manageable task. The result is that you and your partner can basically take the "guesswork" out of the problems or conflicts that present themselves in your relationship, because regardless of whatever specific situations prompt a conflict or upset feelings to begin with (which can be infinite, and often hard to identify), the underlying cause(s) are always just a few (and generally quite easy to identify, once you get the hang of it). Like playing chess with only six moving pieces (three per player), it's a lot easier to see how the whole board fits together.

Chapter Two

Visible Love

You Can't Change What You Can't See

Given that we are in fact provided with sufficient evidence of the Invisible Connection very early in our relationships, one question begs to be asked: why don't we *see* it? If obvious clues are present, ones that provide a clear blueprint for future painful, frustrating conflicts, why do we proceed? Again, it largely comes back to the issue of **mastery**. If one of the primary goals of the unconscious is to overcome previously unmastered childhood experiences with parents, then we *must* find a prospective partner who will offer us opportunities for mastery. If we were to find a person who had none of our parents' negative qualities, there would be no such opportunity. In order to overcome a challenge, there must first be a challenge to overcome.

This is where the Jars come into play. Typically, all human beings will have approximately Three Jars, though some may find it useful to identify more than three. The Three Jars Technique is as follows:

For most of us, our parents' good qualities far outweigh their bad. With that in mind, we could probably construct a much larger list of those qualities that we love and appreciate about them. However, for *this* particular exercise, we will focus only on their less desirable qualities. Take both parents, and identify every single negative aspect of them that you can think of (for some people this is easy, for others it's quite difficult). These can consist of personality or behavior traits, attitudes, habits, lifestyle issues, beliefs, career choices, etc. Take all of those pieces of "data," big or small, and dump them all into a huge vat. Remember—we're not making value judgements or attempting to cast blame; we're just collecting **data**.

Now, take all of that information in the vat, and let it filter down through 100 funnels, 50 funnels, 20 funnels, until you come down to just three funnels, into Three Jars. Those Three Jars will provide you with a blueprint for just about any issue or situation in your life that you would consider to be undesirable or problematic. They will also give you a clear, concise understanding of your Invisible Connection; in other words, the unpleasant traits that you will (unconsciously) be drawn to in a prospective partner...your dysfunctional glue. I will respectfully propose to you that if you look closely enough at any consistent pattern of irritation or conflict in your relationship(s), you will find that one or more of your and/or your partner's Jars will be involved.

The "Three Jars" in a Nutshell

- Every human being has at least two to three core "issues," or areas of sensitivity, that were created in early childhood (primarily age 0-6) as an unavoidable part of the developmental process.

- These sensitive areas result from having certain **principles** repeatedly and consistently "bruised" by parents, though usually unintentionally. This is not a blame thing; it's understanding that patterns of behavior cause patterns of effect. The Jars are essentially the cumulative fallout (in the child) of the parents' own issues. **Parenting is literally an impossible job; the most loving, caring parents will still accidentally create Jars in their children**.

- The Jars create a very specific and predictable **pattern** of reactions (thoughts, feelings, interpretations, and behaviors).

- Outside of traumatic events, virtually any event or situation that produces negative feelings for a person (such as anger, frustration, hurt pride, anxiety, etc.) will have a Jar underneath it. Whenever a person gets irritated, agitated, defensive, takes something personally, or responds with a sense of urgency or passion, it's a dead giveaway that one of their Jars has just been activated.

- The Jars are unconscious. As a result, negative feelings will tend to be seen by the person as being *caused by* the current situation. Most of us would be unaware that much of that subjective feeling is not really about the situation itself, but about the pre-existing Jar. The Jar provides the **power**, the fuel, for the (over)reaction.

- That which is unconscious is not seen, and therefore cannot be controlled. Increasing awareness of the Jars allows for the use of a set of tools to more accurately understand, and better manage, undesirable reactions, feelings, choices, and behaviors.

Jars (choose three)

1. (lack of) attention
2. (lack of) affection
3. (lack of) expression
4. fear/anger
5. loss/abandonment
6. physical neglect
7. fairness
8. respect
9. inconsideration/self-centeredness
10. dependability
11. control
12. irrationality/inconsistency
13. ambivalence/passivity
14. trust/loyalty
15. availability
16. criticism/perfectionism/ self-esteem
17. guilt/obligation/ responsibility
18. closed-mindedness/ rigidity

To clear up any possible confusion, a brief description of each Jar is as follows (detailed Jar worksheets are also provided at the end of the text):

(lack of) attention—parent(s) may or may not have been present, but an overall lack of attention was paid to the child.

(lack of) affection—attention may have been paid, but there was an overall emotional "coolness" to the interaction (such as few "I love yous," hugs, etc.).

(lack of) expression—parent(s) generally kept thoughts and feelings to themselves and had a tendency away from shared, open discussion.

fear/anger—one or both parents generally had a temper or tended to fight or yell frequently or noticeably.

loss/abandonment—parent(s) were completely absent, either through leaving, divorce, or death. Adopted children almost always have this Jar.

physical neglect—children's basic needs for food, shelter, and physical contact/holding were not met.

fairness—children experienced unequal rules or treatment, usually with respect to siblings.

respect—the child's wishes, thoughts, or feelings were somehow minimized or disregarded.

inconsideration/self-centeredness—parent(s) were, for whatever reason, caught up in their own issues to the degree that there wasn't sufficient "room" for the needs of the child to be a priority.

dependability—parent(s) frequently promised to do things but then did not follow through.

control—parent(s) tended to have numerous and/or strict rules, or to tell children how to do things (as opposed to the child being given room to learn for himself or herself). "Over-protective" parenting has the same effect.

irrationality/inconsistency—parent(s) tended to make up random rules, or apply them in a haphazard, uneven manner, or seemed to make illogical/poor choices.

ambivalence/passivity—parent(s) were lukewarm in their responses, or had an overall lack of enthusiasm or self-motivation; at times they may have lacked "backbone."

trust/loyalty—absence or inconsistency of basic trust and honesty, including the withholding of meaningful information from children, unwarranted invasions of privacy, broken promises, or infidelity between parents.

availability—absence of parent(s) through indirect means, e.g., travel, work, alcohol/drug abuse, or disinterest.

criticism/perfectionism/self-esteem—lack of approval, either direct or indirect. Can range from overt insults to implied inadequacies, as well as parent(s) who are perfectionists themselves, e.g., "anal," demanding, etc. Children who are

the victims of any kind of abuse (either verbal, physical, or
sexual) almost always have this Jar.

guilt/obligation/responsibility—may be overt or implied guilt,
demonstrated through statements, tone of voice, looks, or
actions. Oldest children (sometimes referred to as "paren-
tified children") will almost always have this Jar. Often a
result of loss/abandonment.

closed-mindedness/rigidity—inflexible beliefs or rules, or "my
way or the highway," "I know best" kind of thinking.

It's impossible to over-emphasize just how difficult a job
parenting is. In many ways, it's a "no-win situation"; as
mentioned earlier, the most loving, caring, knowledgeable
parents will still unintentionally create Jars in their children. It
is the human condition. The only "Jar-free" option of child
rearing is: don't have children (in much the same way that life
does not offer a "pain-free" option, as regretful as that reality
may at times be). To fully appreciate a parent's challenge,
consider these examples:

fairness—If a family has more than one child (let alone four,
five or more), is it possible for the parents to be 100%
even-handed? If at least one child receives "hand-me-
downs," isn't that child getting unequal treatment? In
addition, first children will necessarily receive different
treatment than subsequent ones, if due to nothing other
than that these parents have never done it before, and will
likely be a little more "freaked out" about the whole experience.

control—What a dilemma...in today's society, what are parents
supposed to do? Be too lenient, and have a spoiled or out-
of-control child; be too strict, and squelch his or her
growth and independence, or prompt them to rebel.

Where is the line? For example, one female client reported that her mother always asked where she was going, with whom, etc. This is considered to be "healthy" parenting. However, as a teenager, she once went to a party, and her mother called her three times to make sure she was okay. Did this have any *real* impact on the daughter? Absolutely; she reported that she never went to another party until she moved out. However, the client also reported that she loved her mother dearly, knew that her mother cared about her very much, and that she did not consider her to be "controlling."

Another client reported an incident in which she was preparing to leave for a week-long business trip, and she indicated to her husband and children that there were prepared meals in the freezer. Her teenage daughter commented, "Controlling, aren't we?" While that may have been true, it could also have been described as nurturing. Obviously, these lines are often quite blurry.

availability—There are many ways in which loving, caring parents can be unavailable to their children, often through no "fault" of their own, but rather due to circumstance. For example, consider the aforementioned two fathers; the one who's an alcoholic, the other who's a surgeon. The alcoholic father is a "functional alcoholic"; he works, supports the family, and is a decent, caring person—he just drinks too much. Nonetheless, society would label his behavior as somewhat "unfavorable." On the other hand, the surgeon is doing something that society would consider quite favorable; industrious, highly educated, and saving people's lives. However, when the little six-year-old daughter is having her first dance recital, and only the mother attends because the father had to cancel at the last minute, it really doesn't matter whether it's because he's intoxicated or saving someone's life. The result is the same to the six-year-old girl, which is: "My father isn't here." While this may be hurtful to her in the moment, it would not cause any relevant damage by itself. However, since these behaviors are generally part of a **pattern**, and will therefore occur many times, they will likely end up creating a Jar around that issue.

criticism/perfectionism/self-esteem—Once again, this issue presents parents with a tremendously challenging balance. Of course, we all want our kids to grow up with skills and abilities in order to be successful. Children cannot achieve these abilities without a certain degree of instruction and correction, which is an unavoidably hurtful process; at the very least, it "stings" a little. Perfectionists are often extremely effective and successful people, and many would hope that their children develop this level of competence.

However, it also often comes with a price; as previously mentioned, I've worked with so many clients of this type that I have begun to refer to it as "successful person's disease." Clearly, this is not a "bad" thing; as with many human characteristics, it is both a wonderful asset as well as, at times, a liability. Perfectionistic parents will tend to "injure" their children's self-esteem thousands of times without meaning to. Although typically these are little, tiny injuries at the instant they occur, they add up over time. This is one of the Jars that's especially "huge" (along with loss, physical neglect, and guilt). There are few (if any) places in a person's life that these particular Jars don't have a significant impact. In my experience, everyone has a least some of the self-esteem Jar.

guilt—This is another of the deep, pervasive Jars. There are many ways in which people can acquire the guilt Jar. It's one (along with criticism/self-esteem/perfectionism) that is prone to injury through both "the front door" and "the back door." The "front door" type of guilt is created by actual, overt statements made by a parent or parents, particularly any kind of direct reference to the child's being the cause of some kind of pain or misfortune for that parent. These would include comments like "I'd be able to ____ if it weren't for you," "You'll be the death of me," "You're giving me gray hair," and "Do you know how much I/we've sacrificed for you?" I've heard actual stories from clients (all basically "normal," everyday people) in which a parent had made statements such as "That's it— I'm gonna throw myself in front of a car!"

The much more prevalent type of guilt, though, is that which comes through the "back door." This occurs either through implication, or simply through circumstance. Tone of voice and facial expressions can convey powerful disapproving, guilt messages. In addition, early childhood loss or trauma (even those that are absolutely no one's fault, such as the death of a parent, divorce, etc.), will almost inevitably result in a guilt Jar. This is due to the fact that young children's brain development (at that time) creates a naturally "ego-centric" perspective, and thus, they will almost unfailingly perceive themselves as being the cause of any major negative event related to the family. This helps to explain why victims of childhood abuse almost always feel personally guilty, even though they themselves were in no way responsible for what happened.

Children will also "absorb" a guilty thought pattern from their parents, even if the parents do not impose any guilt directly on the child/children. For example, one family I worked with had a marked tendency toward self-sacrifice; they were loathe to impose on others in any way, not wanting to "put anyone out." The children in that family inadvertently ended up adopting the parents' belief system. Note: if you notice that someone has a consistent habit of saying "I'm sorry," particularly for things that they really didn't do wrong, like dropping something, crying about something obviously upsetting, etc., it's a *dead giveaway* that they have the guilt Jar.

It is important to note the Jars are neither good nor bad. They may contain many bad *feelings*, and may also be the source of numerous less-than-desirable parts of ourselves, but they also are the basis for many of our greatest strengths, values, and unique and special character traits. **Who** we are is built on the foundation of our Three Jars; they are the **anchor points** for our entire personality makeup. All of the Jars are by definition doubled-edged swords, and have the potential to be both assets and liabilities. In addition, *having* at least three Jars is in no way an insult; to the contrary, if you didn't, it *would* be somewhat of an insult—because it would mean you were dead! **Everyone has at least three Jars**; to say that you do is to say that you have a personality. In other words, everyone has had a childhood filled with experiences that shaped who they are. This is why early life development is referred to as the "formative years." Because these feelings and experiences are so deeply historically embedded in our core makeup, they tend to keep re-surfacing over and over again. As the saying goes, "Those who do not remember history are doomed to repeat it." Therefore, Jars are not to be judged, only *understood*...in order to allow you to make healthier, more effective, and "freer" choices.

By the way, an additional feature of the Jars is that they can "swing both ways," meaning that the possessor of the Jar can be prone to overreacting *to* that issue or behavior when it's displayed, or be prone to *displaying* that behavior him/herself. Thus, a person with the control Jar may be: (a) sensitive to being controlled, (b) controlling, or (c) both. This aspect is not uniform among people with the same Jar(s); it just depends on the individual. As you can see, though, it does create the potential for a certain bit of irony in the fact that a person can be very critical and judgmental toward a principle that they themselves frequently violate...ahh, another paradox built into human nature. More tips on understanding and selecting your Jars can be found at the end of the text.

One of the aspects of the Invisible Connection that may not be immediately obvious is that it gives us the chance to work on our Jars. Since the Jars are both a person's greatest weaknesses and greatest strengths, the fact that we will always find a partner who's good at opening them up can be a blessing in disguise. If you operate under the assumption that one of our purposes in life is to grow, and to overcome our vulnerabilities as much as possible, then confronting the pain in our Jars is essential. Although it's understandable (and normal) not to be thrilled with this prospect, the Invisible Connection, and your partner, will consistently offer you opportunities to strengthen and stretch yourself as a human being.

To this point in the book, most of the content has focused on, for lack of a better way to put it, what's "wrong" with relationships. Clearly, the primary objective of *Irritating the Ones You Love* is to identify common relationship problems and to offer solutions to those problems. However, there's also a tremendous amount that could be written about what's *right* about relationships. To that end, interwoven throughout the remaining text, you will find real stories of real couples who exemplify what it means to be involved in a happy and loving partnership. While conducting much of my professional (and personal) research, I have become a "collector" of great relationship stories. They offer much hope and many lessons, about the relationship process, about what's *possible*, and they exist within a broad spectrum of ages, cultures, and lifestyles.

For example, my grandparents were married for sixty-six years. As relatively amazing as that feat is to begin with, they were also *happily* married. Of course, they dealt with the many ups and downs of life, and with their share of heartaches, but through it all, they were consistently supportive and attentive toward one another. Most importantly, when you asked them about the quality of their years together, they would get tears in their eyes and reply, "I couldn't have asked for a better spouse." Despite many people's cynical view of marriage, and the fashionable idea that somehow relationships can never really succeed in the long run, there are millions of actual couples in the world who offer rock-solid evidence to the contrary. More to come later...

Chapter Three

How to Choose the "Right One"

No Failed Relationships, Only Flawed Selection

Given that we seek love largely in order to bring joy and comfort into our lives, why then do we "choose" people who will consistently irritate us, frustrate us, and possibly hurt our feelings? Because they possess the right combination of **Jars** (i.e., the ones that we inherited from our parents). It offers us an essentially irresistible attraction: to gain control of that which we were unable to control, to overcome those obstacles...to **master** the previously unmastered. I asked one very astute teenage client why she thought people might be so influenced by the pattern of the Invisible Connection to choose the wrong people to date/marry. She thought about it for a moment, and then said, "I don't know...maybe to close up their Jars?" To which I said, "Wow, that's a good answer!" Without this opportunity, much of the underlying purpose of the relationship (from the viewpoint of the unconscious) would be forsaken. To give you an idea how complex human beings are, and the ways in which the two parts of our brains interact, the "conversation" between the conscious and unconscious would go something like this:

(upon the initial meeting, if the Jars are right)

Unconscious (based on almost instant recognition of verbal and nonverbal cues, body language, facial expressions, etc.): "Oh, yeah, this person has just the right type of dysfunction for me to fix!"

Conscious: "Wow, he/she is attractive. Oh, he/she has similar interests to me, is smart, funny, etc. I think maybe I'd like to get to know him/her better."

(upon the initial meeting, if the Jars are wrong)

Unconscious: "Nah, they don't have the right problems/issues for me. There's nothing to be *done* here."

Conscious: "He/she seems perfectly attractive, nice, intelligent and all, but, I don't know...something just doesn't feel right. Something's missing. There's no *chemistry*."

If the couple does begin to pursue a relationship, countless similar internal "conversations" will take place, such as:

Conscious: "Why does he/she do that? It really upsets me/hurts my feelings/makes me angry. I'm not sure if this is a trait/behavior I can tolerate in my partner."

Unconscious: "What are you talking about?? This is *perfect*. If you ditch this person (and these traits/behaviors) now, we'll never get a chance to get them to bend to our will."

Conscious: "Well, you know, it (the undesirable trait/behavior) isn't that big of a deal because (it's the first time, it's not how they normally are, it's such a minor thing, they're just having a bad day, etc.). I really do like/love them anyway, and he/she really does have so many traits I *do* like."

Thus, the unconscious talks the conscious into making the decision to stay and keep trying, and into having fully justifiable reasons for doing so. On the other hand, it should be noted that this need for mastery will only go so far. As I described earlier, human beings are *incredibly* astute in terms of the unconscious' ability to see things with total clarity, things that they themselves may not consciously see. This "radar" is so accurate that I originally called the process the "Magical Connection," due to its "ability" to fit people together in ways that seemed truly unbelievable...almost as if by magic. To wit: one couple had an Invisible Connection around the issue of being "capable." She herself was extremely capable and had a similar need for that in a partner. However, her Invisible Connection's "program" was to draw her to men who were in some way *incapable* (as was one of her parents in certain ways). The man in this case was generally very capable and accomplished, but he had certain aspects of his personality that were "quirky." In addition, the nature of his work did not conform to a 9 to 5 schedule and was therefore somewhat inter-mittent. To her, that added up to be generally the right type of "challenge" to overcome (i.e., a certain amount of this inca-pable quality). **How could her unconscious possibly know all of this enough to be so strongly drawn to him after only a brief initial contact, and vice versa?** This is the power of the unconscious radar; it's so deep that it's a little scary. Every couple I've ever worked with or known has had at least one of these amazingly accurate "dysfunctional fits" as part of the core of their relationship.

However, this particular couple's case illustrates the other side of the coin, which is that when the amount of the dysfunc-tional fit (or *un*fit) is *too* great, the people involved will actually be able to see it and get out. This is where the power of the *conscious* mind comes in, and its ability to recognize when the challenge is simply too large, that the person is "too far under the hump" to ever get over it. In cases such as these, the disparity is large enough to be obvious and undeniable, and the relationship doesn't "stick." Beware, though—the unconscious has a somewhat annoying tendency to more frequently draw us to people who will have **just enough** of this (undesirable) characteristic so that it *will* stick, so that it will *appear* that they'll be able to get over that hump. In other words, they'll be *close enough* to give the realistic impression that they will be able to change sufficiently to satisfy us, and will therefore provide us with the opportunity for mastery.

This results in a feeling that's extremely common for couples, a kind of excruciating frustration that their partner *could* make the necessary adjustments (to meet your needs) if they really wanted to. Thus, the pattern of the Invisible Connection is set into motion, leading to an ongoing cycle, a "push-pull" component to the relationship (as per the previous examples of the internal conscious-unconscious debate). I have not yet met the couple, professionally or personally, that has not had some of these internal conversations at various points in their relationship.

The Perpetual Need for Mastery

One of the dilemmas created by the Invisible Connection is that we are forever in search (unconsciously, unintentionally) of opportunities for mastery, for the ability to "get the better of" previous frustrations, to fix previously "broken" situations (i.e., Jars). As a result, we as human beings have a rather humorous (or excruciating, depending how you look at it!) habit of "chasing our own tails," constantly putting ourselves in situations in which we are trying to get someone or something to conform to our desired version of reality. If you're feeling the need at this point to say, "I don't do that!" remember—this is an **unconscious** process! The 50% visible part of most of us would never allow us to make such ineffective choices. However, the other half, the *invisible* half, is all about making those kinds of "choices"—for some very specific, systematic reasons.

I cannot overstate the power of this pattern. As one very

successful, well put together woman observed (noticing a situation in which she actually became *aware* of her Jars in action, yet continued her behavior anyway): "I can't *believe* how powerful that need (for mastery) is...it's amazing!" From an emotional standpoint, it is the four-year-old child in every one of us that tends to rule this part of ourselves and our behavior. It is not meant at all as an insult to say that this part of all of us is extremely *immature*. Immature literally means *lacking in maturity*, just as you'd expect a four-year-old child to be. Since this is the part of us in which our Jars are so firmly embedded, and which provides the blueprint for each person's particular need for mastery, it is only logical that it's the part of us that comes out when we're in these types of situations. I probably don't have to offer up too much evidence for this assertion...instead, I will simply posit a few questions:

1. Have you ever seen a normally intelligent, calm, rational, successful, and mature adult act like a four-year-old (i.e., having a "temper tantrum," making irrational, emotional statements, crying without explanation, or becoming silent and pouting)?

2. What normally intelligent, calm, rational, successful, and mature adult haven't you seen doing this?

   Examples:
   - A very successful and (normally) professional football coach and executive who "loses it" and screams at his players in an almost hysterical manner, including numerous expletives and personally insulting statements.
   - A highly intelligent and astute television talk show host consistently gets particularly "hot and bothered" when-

ever a certain subject matter comes up on the show.

- A woman who is normally calm and rational when discussing things with her husband (when a particular issue is raised) starts crying and is unable to communicate clearly (and possibly retreats to another room in the house).
- An exemplary employee, normally a model of professionalism and reliability, impulsively violates company policy because his buttons get pushed in an especially effective way by a customer's actions.
- A father who is almost always kind, patient, and supportive when dealing with his daughter consistently reacts with hostility when she does certain behaviors.

I'm providing this *extremely* abbreviated list of examples, because a complete list would be much too long (i.e., six billion people in the world, times __ number for each person...well, you get the idea). These individual cases tell the story well enough for all of us, because they're the *human condition*. Each of us, in our own way, have our own specific, irrational ways of responding to certain situations, be it loudly or silently, publicly or privately. When our Jars are opened up in the right way, we all revert to coping mechanisms that are fundamentally immature and ineffective, but not because we are immature and ineffective *people*—but because certain irreplaceable parts of ourselves become activated in those moments.

These issues are often referred to as "pet peeves"; while true, that term tends to create an impression that the issues are fairly innocent, and therefore can't really be responsible for all *that* much damage (i.e., sort of like pet peeve kittens). To the contrary—in fact, the term **pet peeve dinosaur** would be much more accurate! This term would more realistically

capture the true nature of what's contained in our Jars—
thoughts, feelings, and experiences that are very old and very
large and can be quite primitive and scary, and are often rather
ineffective. They are also part of our own personal history, and,
for better or worse, are incorporated into our makeup. Thus,
while we can't "get rid of" them, we can learn so much about
them (their "history") that we can also learn to manage them
much more effectively.

Learning to Tame Your Pet Peeve Dinosaur

This leads to perhaps the single most important principle
in this text—it is the underlying basis for all of psychology, as
well as every other science or professional discipline (including
medicine, physics, law, sports, accounting, meteorology, engi-
neering, and economics). It can be summed up as such:
**invisible—"it" has the power; visible—*you* have the
power.** When the cause of behavior (thoughts, feelings) is
invisible (unconscious), "it" acts on its own, and you are powerless to control it, because you don't see it to begin with. But
when you've done the work necessary to know your own
patterns well enough, those underlying issues that were invisible start to become *visible* (conscious)—and thus, you begin to
be able to control them... more and more effectively. Therefore,
from a relationship standpoint, one of the most crucial
elements of a happy, healthy, successful partnership is **the
ability to explain and/or understand your own and
your partner's behavior**. *Invisible—"it" has the power;
visible—you have the power.*

Given that all of us have many parts of ourselves that are (at
least initially) invisible, it is no surprise that all of our relationships have many invisible—and therefore somewhat
dysfunctional—dynamics. This is **not** to imply that no relation-

ships are *good* relationships. In fact, many of them are *relatively* happy, healthy, and stable. I use the word relatively not to be negative or cynical, but rather to be precise. As indicated earlier, the completely healthy human being doesn't exist, and therefore neither does the completely healthy couple. On the "relationship continuum," there are many couples for whom the good far outweighs the bad. Although they have their own issues to deal with from time to time, they wouldn't trade each other for the world.

For instance, there's a couple I know well who have been married for thirty-eight years. They spend much of their time together, and willingly choose to share meals and other activities with one another. They obviously get along well and greatly enjoy each other's company. Such is the nature of life; there are always dual realities to any situation. As happy and well balanced as this couple is in the big picture, in the little picture of everyday details, they get on each other's nerves just like anybody else. To illustrate this dual reality a little more clearly, consider their responses to two questions:

1. "Are you happy you're married to each other?" (answer) "Absolutely."
2. "So that means that you never fight?" (laughter) "Of course not! ("What do you mean?") "There are many times where we've thought to ourselves, 'Oh God, at this moment, I don't even *like* you, you're such a (creep, jerk, etc.), I can't believe I've been crazy enough to be married to you for all of these years.' Sure, there are times when I just get so irritated with him, and he with me. And I think any couple who's been married for a while and are honest with themselves will tell you the same thing."

When you hear enough of these kinds of stories, you begin

to realize that they're not so much stories about these *partic-ular* couples, as they are lessons about the human condition. If *these* (wonderful) couples still have Invisible Connections to contend with, what does that mean for everyone else on the continuum? **All** couples will have frustrations and unmet needs to deal with, but the "health" of a relationship will be largely determined by the **degree** and **nature** of those issues. None of these dimensions are exact measurements or values; again, it would be most useful to view them as points, or ranges, on a continuum (for our purposes, with "0" being to the far left and "100" being to the far right).

Degree refers to the balance between the positive and negative parts of the relationship. Although there is no clear objective standard to what "healthy" or "happy" should consist of, it's obvious that it would be preferable to be more toward the right side of the continuum than toward the left. For example, if a couple's relative balance were 50/50, then it would be a frustrating relationship, one marked by inconsistency and ambivalence. Fifty percent "good stuff" is a lot, and would provide the couple with many desirable and joyful experiences together; on the other hand, they would have a fairly large dose of "bad stuff" to contend with as well. This is a difficult type of relationship to be in, because it isn't fully satisfying, and will likely ultimately lead to each partner's not getting his or her needs met sufficiently. However, it may also be a very difficult one to *leave*, because the fifty percent good stuff *does* offer a compelling draw.

In contrast, a couple who has a 75/25 balance would tend to represent the healthier side of the continuum. Twenty-five percent bad stuff is not insignificant, and does contain a fair share of conflict, disappointment, and hurt feelings. However, those frustrations would be a noticeably lesser part of the couple's overall experience with one another. Meanwhile, couples who are clearly on the far *left* of the continuum have relationships marked by a high degree of conflict or lack of communication. Obviously, it would be difficult for individuals in these situations to get their needs met in a satisfying manner, to find any consistent level of joy, or to sustain the relationship in a stable way. While it may, on paper, be hard to understand why anyone would enter into, let alone "choose" to stay in this type of relationship, we also probably all know people who have (possibly even ourselves). The reasons for this will be examined further in the next section.

As far as the **nature** of the relationship is concerned, this would refer to the *type* of issues and conflicts that the couple brings to their partnership. Each individual has their own unique "blend" of personality ingredients, or **dynamics**. One human being's dynamics are complicated enough, but when you start mixing two (or more) people's together, it gets even messier. The combination of these joint dynamics creates what's known as a "fit," which could be "good" or "bad," cooperative or adversarial, constructive or destructive, etc. There are certain types of fit that are more problematic than others.

You Need These Types of Issues and Conflicts Like You Need a Hole in the Head

Persistent—issues that keep coming up over and over, with no effective resolution or progress. Naturally, this would be a very frustrating dynamic to be involved in, and often results in a relationship that has no way to progress (a "dead end"). They may be *willing* to work it out, but unable to due to a fundamental incompatibility built into the relationship. Example: one person is very open and expressive and the other very closed and unemotional. This issue comes up over and over, and despite both of their diligence in attempting to address it, the disparity in their fundamental makeup is simply too great.

Toxic—a volatile mix, the kind that produces highly emotional or bitter arguments.

Abusive—toxic to an extreme enough degree to become violent. Verbal arguments are damaging and hurtful enough, but physically acting out those feelings is a criminal act, period, and is never acceptable.

Passive/Avoidant—individuals or couples who know on some level that there's a serious problem in their relationship, but who can't or won't take active steps to improve the situation. People in these situations often feel "stuck." This type violates one of the most basic tenets of healthy relationships to begin with, which is *mutual growth*. Like "Persistent," these often result in a dead end, because there's an unwillingness or inability to work to get beyond existing problems.

Clueless/Unaware—similar to "Passive/Avoidant," but more extreme. A person or people who are fundamentally unable or unwilling to acknowledge that they have emotional/psychological issues (that are relevant to the situation) to begin with. Therefore, they are unable (or unwilling) to take ownership for their own role in the problem. Since almost all relationship issues are the result of the *interaction* of the two particular people involved, this type leaves little room for resolution of those issues. This dynamic can be summarized by the statement, "It's not me, it's *you*."

These five dynamics cause the nature of the relationship to be so fundamentally unhealthy that they should pretty much be avoided at all costs. They can be thought of as "**dealbreakers**." In relationships, it always "takes two to tango," meaning that there are always two people involved in any relationship pattern. However, it is possible for one person to be the **primary** violator (or perpetrator, e.g., in the case of abuse). It depends on the couple, and the specific people involved. So, for any of the above dynamics, it may be that one or both people are primarily responsible for the continuation of the pattern. For instance, one or both partners could have a volatile temper and/or a tendency to resort to physical violence; one or both partners could be unaware of and unwilling to address their own psychological/emotional issues; one or both partners could be unwilling/unable to let an issue go after it had seemingly been sufficiently resolved, etc.

You may have noticed that couples with these particular patterns of communication are not fighting about anything that's particularly *unique*. In other words, their disagreements are still about the same basic topics as all other couples, e.g., fairness, trust, dependability, etc. What is unique about them though is the **degree** of their differences, or the **method** in which they go about addressing those differences. The method used to communicate and resolve complaints will have a major impact on its success or failure. It's not necessarily that there *are* issues to deal with in the relationship, but *how* they're dealt with—the method can make all the difference in the world, as will be described in detail in the final chapter. However, as mentioned several times throughout this text, great methods will almost never be sufficient to overcome fundamentally incompatible ingredients.

The Relationship Trap:
Being Blinded by Your Invisible Connection

As many people have experienced, disentangling yourself from a relationship can be much easier said than done, especially when intense feelings such as love, affection, intimacy, and commitment are involved. In addition, simply having shared so much history and experience with someone can produce an intense feeling of closeness and loyalty. As much as these elements all play a substantial role in the pain involved in the breakup process, none of them are ultimately as powerful as the Invisible Connection. In terms of sheer *stickiness*, the Invisible Connection has no rival.

Given a high **degree** and/or **nature** of incompatibility, it would appear that it would be obvious to that couple and to those who know them that their relationship isn't going to work out, nor should it, because its inherent problems clearly outweigh its' benefits. Nonetheless, though presented with indications of visible problems from the beginning, it's extremely common for people to pursue relationships that they "shouldn't," or stay in them longer than they "should." Many people may have known a couple about which they say to themselves, "These two people aren't very happy; they seem to drive each other crazy. Why the heck are they still together?"

As mentioned earlier, the attraction of the Invisible Connection is very powerful, very *sticky*. The opportunity to right previous wrongs, to gain mastery over the unmastered, is one that's so precious that it will lead us to pursue paths that we otherwise would not. If the choice of a partner were solely up to the conscious brain, then relationships would almost always work out successfully and permanently. We would simply wait until we found a person with the desirable traits we wanted who had no major destructive flaws, and we would live happily ever after. However, actively competing with that conscious agenda are the goals of the *unconscious*, much of which, as you know by now, is to find a person who possesses the negative issues (Jars) from our childhood, so that we can re-create the child-parent dynamic, and come out on top.

Unfortunately, that's not a very positive, light-hearted goal. In order for it to be met, we must find someone who will re-create **conflict** with us. This is not a very appealing thought, and would take a lot of the fun and excitement out of the dating process. So, given that the **un**conscious is in fact unconscious, we are simply not aware of its agenda, nor its *methods*. One of its primary methods is to, essentially, "trick" us into consciously believing something that's not true. For instance, a person with a fear of abandonment (the loss/abandonment Jar) is someone who would crave stability in a relationship. Theoretically, they would seek out another person who craves stability, and both would get their needs met. However, what happens much more frequently is that the *unconscious* agenda wins out, so that they will instead find a person who's elusive, who tends to run from commitment. This provides the person with the valuable opportunity to get the other person to *stop* running, to *become* stable.

Since this behavior trait (elusiveness) would be an obviously undesirable one for the person with the loss Jar, and given that we're always presented with some type of clear evidence of the existence of these key traits, logic would dictate that the first person would quickly lose interest and move on. But, typically, we don't. We will stay and "fight," to try to win, to master. In order to do this, we cannot see the unwanted traits clearly. So, the unconscious tricks us into: (a) **not** seeing things we need to see (filtering *out* information), and, (b) seeing things that **aren't there** (filling *in* information). The unconscious frequently **blinds** us from seeing, or into seeing, highly relevant information about prospective partners.

The human mind has an incredible way of "filling in the blanks." This is true in many different situations, not just with respect to relationships. For instance, in the legal field, it's a fact that "eyewitness" testimony is a highly unreliable source of information, because, while someone may have actually witnessed an event, people also tend to "see what they want to see." Our perceptions, feelings, and experiences are based on a combination of factual information and subjective **interpretation**. Although we're often able to rely primarily on objective facts when it comes to issues related to business, science, finance, health care, etc., when it comes to love and interpersonal relationships, human beings' judgments tend to become much less reliable.

Part of the reason for this is that the human brain is designed in such a way as to not require a complete set of facts in order to function. This has a highly adaptive value in that it allows us to assess many situations more quickly and act accordingly without a prolonged examination process. For instance, in a medical emergency, a physician may make an initial diagnosis and take an immediate course of action based on a relatively cursory impression of the patient's condition. The doctor's speed, in this case, could mean the difference between life and death. His or her assessment, though *based* on observable facts, may be largely filled in by previous experience and existing knowledge.

Thus, in medical, financial, and business situations, "educated guesses" are a reliable part of the decision-making process, because they're based on concrete, observable data (e.g., numbers, statistics, blood pressure, heart rate, etc.). However, *emotional* issues are largely **internal**, and are therefore *not* (easily) observable or measurable; they are largely **hidden**. In fact, the term "personality" is derived from the Latin word *persona*, or "mask." Thus, in matters of the heart, we must rely even more heavily on sources of information that are largely subjective.

As previously noted, we are blinded *from* seeing things that *are* there and *into* seeing things that *aren't*. These inaccuracies are necessary in order to be able to "fall in love," have relationships, and perpetuate the human race. If we were to be fully aware immediately of the total picture of a prospective partner, including all of their blemishes and quirks and undesirable habits, it's hard to imagine any two people sticking around past a few dates. This would be extremely maladaptive. As is so often the case, a behavior pattern can be both an asset and a liability, depending on the situation. The blindness helps us to form sustained and potentially lifelong relationships and create families. It allows us to find people who have the right Invisible Connection, who will give us the chance to master issues from our childhood. And it frequently causes us to put ourselves into situations that turn out to be painful and frustrating.

Seeing Clearly Means Looking for the Right Things

Unfortunately, there is no magic formula to picking the right partner. Putting aside numerous intangibles such as luck, fate, destiny, timing, the right place at the right time, etc., there are several more concrete, predictable issues to pay attention to. Notice that I said "**pay attention to**," and not control or fix. Because the unconscious is so heavily involved in all of these issues, we aren't free to make 100% unclouded decisions. However, the whole point of this book is that we *are* free, if we choose, to make more *well-informed* decisions. In order to do that, we first have to know what we're looking for.

The first is to pay attention to what **is** there that you aren't seeing. In some ways, this part is no "mystery"; it is the Invisible Connection. Thus, the nonmystery part is that you can anticipate fully that it **will** be there; the mystery part is that it is still **invisible** (or, at least, knowing what you know now, not *fully* visible). Given that the unconscious is specifically motivated to find certain undesirable traits in potential partners (our Three Jars), we will tend to be most blind to seeing those particular characteristics. Our Three Jars essentially act as a "filter," screening out unpleasant information and allowing through only the parts that we *want* to see so that we can continue the quest for mastery. Ironically, the underlying issues that tend to draw us to a person the most are the very things that may eventually cause us the greatest pain. In the vast majority of relationships that eventually end, the true, core issues that cause the breakup are ones surrounding the Invisible Connection, even though it's common for people to attribute it to more visible problems such as money, lack of passion or intimacy, or having "drifted apart."

For example, if a woman has a "dependability" Jar, then what she needs and wants most from a partner is that he be dependable. Common sense would dictate that she would consistently seek out men who are reliable; however, this is almost never the case. Instead, she will be drawn to men who in some way, shape, or form cannot be counted on, like one (or both) of her parents. Consciously, she knows she doesn't want this trait; unconsciously, she's seeking to re-create that familiar scenario so that she can gain control over it. It truly is a "booby trap" built into human nature. Therefore, the first step you can take to begin to modify this pattern is to **know your Three Jars like the back of your hand**. You can count on the fact that you **will** find people who possess the right ingredients to open them up; people's "radar" for these traits tends to be extremely accurate.

Developing X-Ray Vision

Learning to see what would be invisible to most people is a skill; it can be learned, but you have to work at it, and know what to look for. This can be very tricky at first, until you get the hang of it, because people typically display their "best behavior" in the early stages of a relationship, and will therefore usually only reveal their undesirable traits in subtle ways. If these quirks were more blatant (which in some cases they are), they would be much easier to identify. For instance, one client told me of an experience in which he met a woman who appeared very interested in him, and asked him to call her.

When he did, she was unable to talk, so said she would call him back later that day. A week went by, and no phone call. Finally, he called her again, and politely asked why she hadn't called back. At that point, she basically "went off," saying, "I don't have to answer to you! You don't know what my week was like! How dare you make such an accusation!" Given that one of his Jars was "irrationality," it didn't take much for him to realize that she was not the person for him. She basically smacked him over the head with that Jar, so he couldn't miss it (although sometimes people still do). Incidentally, the level of *her* (over)reaction clearly illustrates what often happens when a person's Jars are activated.

Much more frequently, however, the clues will be revealed in bits and pieces, and may seem to be more like "accidents" than consistent traits. This is where the "blindness" comes in, the interference that's caused by the unconscious. As a result, people will frequently rationalize or make excuses for the unwanted traits and behaviors they *do* see. Typically, those traits and behaviors will turn out to be relevant, because human beings tend to be very predictable in this regard. In other words, when it comes to a person's basic, core personality, individual behaviors that happen **consistently** will reveal genuine information about that person as a whole.

For instance, a person who displays a pattern of erratic decision-making *is* a person who makes irrational decisions. A person who has a consistent history of infidelity *is* a person who cheats. A person who frequently makes commitments that they don't keep *is* someone who's unreliable. A person who typically finds something wrong with whatever you do *is* critical. While this may not always be true, it is the vast majority of the time. When it comes to consistent patterns of behavior, people *are* how they *act*, especially in romantic relationships.

So the first two keys to developing your X-Ray Vision (and

therefore selecting a compatible partner) are **pay attention to what you see**, and **don't disregard it when you see it** ... as that information will almost always turn out to be useful. In "normal" people (i.e., not suffering from a specific, diagnosable mental disorder), I have found that the second biggest cause for "failed" relationships is **disregarded information** (the first, as previously mentioned, is unwillingness to struggle and work through issues). This doesn't mean that anytime you see any indication of your Jars in a potential partner that you should immediately terminate the relationship; in fact, it's inevitable that you *will* see evidence of it. The crucial step is what you *do* with it when you see it. This is where the aforementioned issues of **degree** and **nature** come into play. Seeing these dynamics clearly allows you to assess them further and make informed choices, i.e., how much of this person's total makeup is influenced by these characteristics? Is their version of these behaviors one that you can live with in the long run? What is the nature of these traits: relatively mild (benign), or severe (toxic)?

For example, if the Jar that's involved is "anger," then there's a range of ways in which a person could display that anger. They could pound their fist on a table and yell (toxic), they could become silent and refuse to communicate (dead end), or they could clearly state their complaint, albeit in an angry tone of voice (reasonably benign). The person in all three cases is expressing legitimate feelings, but only the latter is doing it in a way that allows for some constructive solution. People often comment (when they truly get the Invisible Connection concept), "You mean I'm stuck with this? I'm always gonna find someone who's (controlling, unavailable, unreliable, etc.)?" I'd *like* to say "no," but the answer really is "yes"...albeit with a very important "but." You may be stuck with your Jars and your Invisible Connection, but you *can* find a truly good (benign) version of it.

The development of your X-Ray Vision can save you a lot of unnecessary heartache. For instance, a client recently told me of a potential new love interest of hers in which the man misrepresented his career status (something akin to "owner" of a company versus "assistant manager"). This is a relevant piece of information, not to be disregarded. Of course, her natural inclination was to minimize or rationalize it ("I figured he was only trying to impress me"). However, these types of behaviors are more often what I call "**tips of an emotional iceberg**"; they may seem inconsequential, but they are only a small part of what lies underneath. On the other hand, it would be unfair and rigid to dismiss someone on the basis of only one piece of undesirable information. Therefore, I recommend the use of a reasonable yet reliable standard: three strikes and you're out. When you see something that significantly concerns you once, you say, "hmm"; when you see it twice, it begins to indicate a pattern; when you see it three times, it's extremely likely that that's *who* that person *is*. Given that the woman had a clear trust Jar, the information she was seeing was likely to be part of a potentially damaging Invisible Connection.

Another great example was provided by a man who was on a first date with a woman to whom he was very "attracted," both physically and emotionally. One of the ingredients that he knew was most important for him to find in a partner was for her to be very open and expressive with her emotions. Several times throughout their initial conversation on the date, she made reference to an upsetting situation she had been dealing with, and that she had "refused" to cry over it, even though she felt those feelings. To her, it was more important to be able to conceal those emotions, to be "strong." The man reported having actually *noticed* this characteristic, and felt himself bristle a bit when she made these comments. So, he was actually *aware* of this being an area to be concerned about—it was a red flag, a potential "deal-breaker." Despite these visible signs, his unconscious quickly talked him out of giving credence to this information. Over and over his mind kept coming back to this issue, and over and over he kept disregarding his uneasy feeling, saying to himself, "It's not that big of a deal—she's probably not really like that. I have to give her a chance." In other words, his Invisible Connection was unmistakably in motion, setting him up for the potential, valuable opportunity to master this behavior in a loved one—as well as the potential to be consistently frustrated and hurt by it, to not be able to get **his particular emotional needs met by this particular woman** (which ultimately proved to be the case).

To clarify this a bit further, each couple's **nature** will have its own unique "fit," which will largely be a function of their own specific combination of Jars. One very useful rule of thumb is that, generally speaking, it is better for the fit (or unfit) between your and your partner's Jars to be **indirect rather than direct**. The unavoidable makeup of the Invisible Connection means that you *will* find someone who will open up and irritate your Jars. However, it's not necessary for this to be done in the harshest or most severe manner. Simply put, the more direct (or antagonistic) the fit of Jars is, the more severe the opening of them will be.

For example, let's say one person's biggest Jar was irrationality, which in this case made her very sensitive to irrational behavior. Obviously, if she were to marry a man who had the same Jar, but that swung in the other direction (meaning that he was prone to irrational behavior), it would set up a pattern in which they would be rubbing salt in each other's wounds in the most direct manner possible—or more like *grinding* salt in those wounds. On the other hand, if she were to choose a man who had the control Jar instead (and control was not one of her other Three Jars), it would not be directly irritating. In this case, his controlling behavior would *at times* present itself in what may seem to her to be an irrational way, but it wouldn't be a "direct hit" as much as it would be a "glancing blow." While still annoying, over the long haul it was a **degree** of annoyance that was tolerable to both of them, and therefore didn't threaten the overall happiness or stability of the relationship. To summarize, given that we do tend to "marry our mother/father," as the saying goes, better to marry a *partial* version vs. an *exact* one!

So, seeing the Invisible Connection for what it is allows you to make more accurate assessments of potential partners, and allows you to better predict the longterm compatibility of a relationship. Likewise, seeing what's *missing* provides a useful body of information as well. As previously mentioned, our brains tend to fill in those missing parts with the traits that we would *like* to see. Obviously, no one wants to think of his or her partner as being deficient in any important way; we may want to think of them as being smart, or funny, or charming, or sensitive, or creative, or deep, or caring. Can you imagine saying, "Yeah, this is the love of my life, she's kind of superficial, but I love her anyway," or, "This is the man I plan to marry...I know he's kind of obnoxious, but he's still great."

Few of us would want to think of someone we deeply care about in this manner. So, the mind "fills in the blanks." We will tend to minimize characteristics that we don't like, and maximize the ones that we do. For instance, an associate of mine, while describing her husband, mentioned that he's a very "happy-go-lucky" type of person, which she was citing as an example of what a pleasure he was to be around. However, in the same discussion, the issue was raised that he often seems unable to discuss problems with her on a deeper level when necessary. This unwillingness to "argue" often resulted in important issues going unresolved. While she was clearly happy with him as a partner overall, this particular aspect of their relationship often left her feeling unsatisfied. Even though she knew of this trait early on, she saw only part of it. As is so common, she "filled in" the rest with something that she wanted to see.

On one hand, this is a totally normal and, in fact, unavoidable human tendency. On the other hand, it causes us to have, at least to some degree, a **distorted** view of our partner. On one hand, these distortions are necessary, because, in order to maintain a happy and healthy relationship, we must see them in a favorable light. On the other hand, in order to maintain a happy and healthy relationship, we must see them **accurately**. The distortions protect us from painful or unpleasant information, but they also block us from getting our needs met, as well as growing, in the fullest manner possible (a state that may be referred to as "true love").

You Can't Get What You Want
If You Don't Know What "It" Is

Achieving the ideal balance is not easy (and probably not even possible), but there are some ways to increase your skill in this area. First, it's helpful to know what *you* truly want and need in a partner, particularly those things that you would define as *indispensable*. While it's extremely unlikely to find someone who matches your preferred makeup completely, it is possible to find someone who offers you *enough* of those qualities. These will typically consist of things such as:

• interests (hobbies, tastes)

• lifestyle ("speed" of life, i.e., casual, fast-paced, hard-driving, night or morning)

- values (priorities, beliefs, commitment to growth)

- emotional style (warm, open, sensitive, empathic, cool, defensive, stoic, intolerant)

- intellectual style (level of intelligence, complex or simple, esoteric or concrete)

- energy level (hyper vs. needs a lot of sleep)

- personal habits (rigid or flexible, quirky or not, high or low maintenance)

- motivation level (willingness to try, put forth effort)

- problem-solving style (active or passive, systematic or random, internal or external)

- career orientation (work to live or live to work, employee or entrepreneur)

- social style (gregarious or private, introvert or extrovert)

- approaches to diet and fitness (way of life, casual interest, etc.)

- verbal style (talkative, expressive, quiet, reserved)

- sexual appetites and preferences (frequency, wild or conservative, etc.)

- physical appearance (low priority, obsession, etc.)

- sense of humor (dry, silly, consistent, occasional)

- attitude (positive, negative, hopeful, pessimistic)

- financial goals (money/possessions as major priority, just want enough to live, etc.)

- spiritual or philosophical viewpoints (deep and explorative, surface and tangible)

- religious orientation (type, practicing or not, etc.)

- political views (liberal, conservative, socially conscious, self-oriented)

- temperament (uptight or easy-going, snuggly or squirmy, needy or self-reliant, loud or quiet)

- family orientation (kids—yes or no, how many, who will raise them)

- couple orientation (closeness vs. distance, shared time vs. independent activity)

- cooperation (willingness, ability, mutual or one-sided, comfort/easiness)

For a particular person, several of these may hold special significance, while others may be of only mild or moderate value. In order to choose a partner most effectively, you must first know your own position on these issues. Is this merely a "preference," or is it a "passion"? Is it something you'd like (but can do without), or is it a "must have"? For example, someone who thrives on fitness doesn't belong with a person who couldn't care less about exercise. Someone who loves travel and the outdoors shouldn't choose a "homebody." Someone who's favorite activity is snuggling on the couch and watching movies together shouldn't be with someone who's easily bored and always has to be "doing something," etc.

These criteria are not meant to be an impersonal "check-list," but rather a guide, a way to more consciously look at and understand the ingredients that may give you the most fulfilling and successful relationship. They are not intended to take the romance out of the relationship process—of course, it is possible to overdo anything, even a good thing. However, the "magic" of falling in love will always have some element of mystery and excitement to it, regardless of what information we use to try to make more informed choices. Generally, this system is best used in a *balanced* way, in which thoughtfulness is introduced in the process, while still allowing the process to unfold reasonably naturally. However, as one woman contemplated this approach, it suddenly occurred to her, "It's really a lot like a job interview." Exactly. Imagine interviewing for a job, but one in which the clear understanding was that it was to be your absolute *last* job...you would be signing a contract that said you would be at this job, as your one and only, until the day you die. Would you say, "Oh well, I don't know *that* much about it, but it seems pretty good to me. Okay, I'll take it"? No way! Most people would become incredibly meticulous, asking every conceivable question of the prospective employer, covering every angle, trying to anticipate every possible pitfall. After all, this is your last job *ever*. "Hmm...perhaps I'd like a second interview, please!"

The other tip for improving your ability to choose wisely is to notice yourself regularly giving up your wants and needs with a potential partner. If you find yourself consistently being disappointed, feeling unappreciated or unrecognized, or doing a lot of your activities solo (not by choice), then it's probably happening for a reason. In general, when you have to "drag" your partner into doing an activity with you that *you* love, it's telling you something about the baseline level of compatibility, or lack thereof, in the relationship.

This leads to an important distinction. In a perfect world, we would get all of our wants and needs met completely with one partner. However, establishing a real and mature relationship means that it will include some (and possibly *many*) imperfections. That's why it's so important to know for yourself what you really want and need in a relationship. Once again, it's helpful to apply a continuum to this criteria. Some things you may feel are of little consequence, and you simply won't mind them, even if they're "undesirable." Some things you may feel you must have in order to be fully satisfied with your partner. However, often there isn't one set "point" for a particular quality, but rather more of a **range**. I have found that for these types of issues, it's useful to think in terms of a "ballpark." Specifically, are they "in the ballpark" of the particular attribute(s) that you're looking for?

While the person may not be *exactly* what you want in a particular area, they can still be truly "good enough" (although this would depend on the issue in question). For instance, they may not have the identical interests and hobbies that you do, but theirs is similar enough to your own to be compatible. Their sexual appetite may not be totally equal to yours, but it's close enough to be mutually satisfying, etc. "In the ballpark" means that you can work with it, and find satisfaction together; "out of the ballpark" means that the disparity is too great, and you or your partner would have to be something that you're not. For example, if one person is passionate about art, and loves going to museums and exhibits, and the other just doesn't have any interest, then one of them is going to consistently end up feeling either disappointed or put out. This type of match-up creates a situation in which it's more or less a "chore" to share in a favorite activity, which tends to suck a lot of the joy out of the relationship over time.

Learning to Avoid Putting Round Pegs in Square Holes

If you find that one (or both) of you have to stretch to your limit just to fit together, it's not in the ballpark. If people have to essentially twist themselves into a pretzel in order to find common ground, the fit just isn't right. As you can see, this is not an exact science; it's simply a tool that you can use to help you make more informed choices about a prospective partner. While there is no clear-cut standard, you can try using this four-part guideline to assist you. Remember—these are based on your own subjective definition of what's important to *you*:

1. "irrelevant"
2. "would be nice if, but not important"
3. "important, but not essential"
4. "essential"

But what about the old idea that "opposites attract"? Well, yes, it's often true that differences do create feelings that are immediately intense and appealing. However, they're also likely to be a recipe for disaster. To clarify, differences in general are not necessarily a problem, but extreme differences, especially in important or essential areas, usually are. For instance, if one person loves reading and the other prefers watching TV, that's probably not a big deal. But if one person enjoys having open, deep, philosophical discussions, while the other prefers to keep things light and superficial, it's likely that that discrepancy will eventually become a source of conflict and/or unmet need in the relationship.

Initially, differences may provide a "spark" to a relationship, and often will make it seem more interesting (a phenomenon also known as "chemistry"). While it's possible for a couple to continue to feel this way, more often (especially over time) that "spark" loses its appeal, and the fact that they're unable to share in an important area becomes consistently disappointing. Opposites may in fact *attract*, but usually not in a good way; there's many a divorced couple whose story started with this rationalization.

So, by using the four-part guideline, you can better assess whether your differences are likely to be complementary or antagonistic. A particularly frustrating and perplexing aspect of this match-up process, and of the Invisible Connection, is that people may have a major imbalance between them that gets persistently overlooked because they simply *want* the relationship to work out. The expression "Love conquers all" may often be true for couples who are trying to cope with the unavoidable challenges of a partnership that was built on a solid foundation of compatibility to begin with. But "love" usually cannot compensate for a poor match-up...regardless of how strong the couple's feelings of affection and caring are. In other words, love usually *cannot* conquer bad ingredients (likewise, a carefully prepared cake made with high quality chocolate and fresh asparagus will probably not result in a combination that works).

Consider two trapeze artists; both are skillful, fit, and highly motivated. They both *want* to join hands, and are both *trying* as hard as they can to meet each other in the same place. However, success or failure will be determined less by how much they want to hook up and more by where they are both "jumping off from" to begin with. Imagine them both stretching, reaching, with all of their might, but, having started from locations that were just too far apart, unable to connect. This is an extremely common dilemma in relationships, and one that is very painful. The *desire* may be there, but they just keep "missing" each other. This is the Invisible Connection in action, and although all couples have this dynamic to some degree, it usually ends up being a deal-breaker if the degree is too great.

People Are Who They Are, Not Who We Want Them to Be

One of the problems with much of the relationship process being driven by the unconscious is that it tends to lead us into a "trap" of seeing a partner based largely on **fantasy** rather than **reality**. Frequently, people will generalize specific desirable aspects of the person, and use those parts as a basis for the entire relationship. This illuminates one of the most common relationship traps, which is that **the whole is always *made***

73

up **of parts, but the parts don't necessarily make up a whole**. For instance, one client found his partner's habit of consistently letting him down to be hurtful and frustrating. She would make plans with him and then cancel them, or at times would just not show up at all. In addition, she would often add insult to injury by avoiding all contact with him for days afterward. Clearly, this type of behavior would be unacceptable to many people, and they would simply terminate the relationship; it would qualify as a "deal-breaker." Although on one level (the *visible* one) he recognized this as a major problem, it was also one of his Jars (dependability), and thus was a core part of his *Invisible* Connection. His unconscious kept duping him, over and over, into believing her behavior would change.

As a result, he would persistently justify the "rightness" of the relationship by referring to some of her more desirable traits ("I feel so good when I'm with her, no one's ever made me laugh like her," etc.). The problem is that her wonderful sense of humor did not make up for her lack of dependability. This is the trap; the belief that certain **parts** are sufficient to make a **whole**. That *could* be true, but it isn't necessarily; it depends on the parts. In his partner's case, her sense of humor may have been a genuinely enjoyable trait, but it paled in comparison to the fact that she deeply wounded him repeatedly by being unreliable. Clients have told me hundreds of examples of these kinds of erroneous assumptions, that one particular aspect indicates that the person is the "right one" for them, because, for instance:

- they were adventurous and fun-loving (but weren't trustworthy)
- they were steady and reliable (but couldn't openly communicate)
- they were loving and sensitive (but made irrational decisions)
- they were rational and efficient (but were critical and demanding)

▪ they were a loving parent and provider (but had an unpre-
  dictable temper)

In these and infinite other cases, the desirable quality was
viewed as being one of the primary features on which the entire
relationship could be based. While that's not necessarily
untrue, it is when other, more crucial features are overlooked
or minimized as a result. This would be much like an emergency room physician treating a patient's broken leg while he
or she was in cardiac arrest; it's a matter of *priorities*. In each
of the above examples, the positive trait was in fact (all things
being equal) a quality that would enhance the relationship.
However, the *negative* trait was one that had the ability to *ruin*
it. How can you tell the difference? Again, it's a matter of priorities. In these cases, the negative characteristics were all ones
that matched the partner's Jars, and were therefore more relevant, because they were part of the Invisible Connection. For
instance, in the first example above, while the adventurous
quality was lots of fun to be around, it was more or less a bonus
("important, but not essential"). On the other hand, the issue of
trust, being one of the client's Jars, was "essential," and was
therefore big enough to be a deal-breaker.

The irony is that when couples have difficulty in their relationships (i.e., ones that are persistent, that threaten the
continuity, etc.), it is virtually always due to *these issues* that
were present from the beginning. Human beings have an
amazing tendency to keep getting disappointed by their partners when they do the things that they've *always done*.
Therefore, if you "choose" someone who's not trustworthy, it's
shouldn't be a big surprise that their behavior will continue to
be untrustworthy. If you "choose" a person who's critical, you
shouldn't expect them to start being more tolerant. For the
most part, people's **character** does not change. People *are*

capable of amazing growth when it comes to making *adjustments* or *improvements* in their attitudes and behavior, but generally do not alter their **basic nature or makeup**. Those core characteristics are analogous to a boat's rudder; if it's set in a particular direction, the whole boat will ultimately keep getting pulled toward that direction. To expect a partner to circumvent this process is to expect them, literally, to be someone they're not.

However, this is a hallmark of the Invisible Connection in action, because, as previously stated, the underlying pull (like an undertow) of this pattern comes from very deep, powerful feelings toward parents. A major aspect of why it's often so painful for couples to pull themselves apart from each other in order to end a relationship is because of this underlying parent connection. It cannot be overstated how strong this dynamic is. If the dysfunctional glue that tugs so much at your heart is largely because this person is **representing** your parents, and the hope that *they'll* love you exactly how you always wanted them to, then how are you going to give up on *that*? No wonder the thought of ending a relationship provokes such terribly painful feelings for so many people; it's literally as if you're breaking up with your **parents** (at least from the perspective of your unconscious). Imagine how a six-year old child would feel about having to terminate their relationship with their parents...now *that's* pain.

In addition, there's also a great deal of genuine pain associated simply with losing all of the benefits that come with having a longterm relationship. Elements such as countless shared experiences and history, common bonds, intertwined details of everyday life, memories of holidays and other special occasions—in many ways, these become part of who both you and your partner *are*. Because these things all have powerful feelings attached to them, such as love, affection, trust, understanding, and mutual respect, it may feel for many people as if a part of them is being ripped out from the inside. As almost all people know (maybe more than they'd care to), this process can feel excruciatingly painful and sad. As will be discussed further in the final chapter, part of this pain is legitimately about the *real* loss of the *real* partner, and part of it is about the deeper psychological loss associated with the Invisible Connection. Given that both are at play, it's very understandable that people often have trouble walking away from a relationship.

So, as adults, we find ways of avoiding that pain, of ratio-nalizing a partner's behavior or undesirable characteristics. It's also common for people to make a kind of funny assumption about others that their good points are real and solid, whereas their bad points are somehow optional and easily changed. It's not often easy for us as human beings to tolerate all of the gray-ness in people, to see them as a whole, with an inextricable mixture of both positive and negative features.

I'm not saying there shouldn't be any undesirable behav-iors or traits in your partner. If there weren't, they wouldn't be human. I'm talking about specific *types* of behaviors or charac-teristics; ones that are either deal-breakers, dead-ends, too painful, or simply incompatible. The presence of these partic-ular types of issues strongly suggests that the relationship is one that cannot be worked out, no matter how hard the couple tries or wants it to, because the two people involved are just not sufficiently well-matched.

20/20 Hindsight May Be Good, But 20/20 Foresight Is Better

In order to avoid being forever disappointed (hurt, frus-trated, angered, etc.) by your partner's actions, you must **choose a person who has what you want to begin with**. I recently heard someone say (who's happily married), "The first rule of marriage is: marry someone who wants to be married to you." As obvious as this may sound, it's amazing how often people don't do it. Competing with this simple yet wise philosophy is the Invisible Connection, the essence of which is: **find someone who has some fundamental characteristic(s) you don't want, and get them to change**. If the person you choose is outside the ballpark of any feature that's crucial to you, it's extremely unlikely they'll ever change enough to get inside that ballpark. While people will often make these types of changes *temporarily*, they rarely stick; people almost never stop being who they **fundamentally are**.

Fortunately, there are billions of people in the world to choose *from*. In addition, one of the great advantages to people remaining who they fundamentally are is that they won't be able to *hide* who they fundamentally are. This is a very helpful aspect of human nature, and I cannot emphasize the importance of this statement enough: **a person will always "tell" you what you need to know** (about them). Whatever information you need to make educated, healthy choices in the dating world, you'll get. The question is, *will you be listening*? Remember—your unconscious is motivated to try to "trick" you into missing this information, so you'll need to use as much of your conscious brain as possible. Since the unconscious brain runs "interference" with our ability to see clearly, we must use our conscious brain (knowledge, information, tools, and effort) to run interference *back*.

This is where the invisible and visible parts of our experience come together. You can maximize your ability to see clearly by applying this simple principle: **the invisible will always be revealed by the visible**. Therefore, the aspects of a person that may be largely "hidden" initially will still be exposed by some observable behaviors (e.g., tips of emotional icebergs). What may appear to be innocent, inconsequential actions, when viewed one at a time, are usually *microcosms* of more fixed personality traits of that individual. Human beings rarely do anything "just because." Except for the occasional random impulse, human beings tend to be very *consistent* in their actions. A person's character is almost always stable over time because it's part of a lifelong *system* of behavior. So, people will reveal their deep, basic personality traits (or Jars) through their **actions** (in fact, often with just *one* action). For example:

- A person will pick up something that you put down and move it somewhere slightly different (perfectionism).

- Someone will tell you they'll call at a specific time and don't without explanation (dependability).

- A person will tell you (without your asking) exactly how you should do something (control).

- At a restaurant, someone will get noticeably annoyed when the waiter gets some aspect of their order wrong (respect).

- You ask your date to pass you the pepper, and they (unnecessarily) say, "Oh, sorry" (guilt).

- Your date seems to go out of their way to point out their assets, e.g., how much money they have, how popular they are, etc. (self-centeredness).

- The person has noticeable difficulty making any kind of firm decision about plans for the date (ambivalence).

- They say that they're definitely interested in going out with you, but it takes them two weeks to find an open time in their schedule (availability).

- While driving to your destination, the person suddenly jerks the car to get around traffic (anger).

By the way, these examples, and hundreds of others like them, are of things that typically occur very early in the dating process, often on the first date. As irrelevant as they may seem, these kinds of concrete behaviors provide a quick and reliable "glimpse" of that person's basic personality trait(s); they can be viewed as a *blueprint*. Of course, there's nothing necessarily wrong with any of these traits; they're all part of what make up normal human behavior. However, remember that we tend to be drawn to particular people not by accident, but by design. Therefore, these characteristics will be *highly* relevant if they're similar to *your* Jars (and thus your Invisible Connection). So, don't overlook them—they're most likely telling you something very important about who that person is, and, more importantly, who they will remain.

Does this mean that you should pick apart everything that a person does? How do you tell the difference between being hypercritical and paying attention? Part of the joy of dating is a naturally unfolding process of discovery, and I wouldn't want to encourage people to "work at it" to the point that they ruin it. Fortunately, it's usually not necessary to do this, because you won't have to look that hard. If they're deal-breaker issues, **they'll find you**. However, it's important to distinguish between **macro** and **micro** issues. Macro issues are broad, core aspects of the person or the relationship; they are patterns, Jars. Micro issues are specific details of the person or relationship. Focusing on or obsessing about micro issues will tend to prevent you from finding a genuine partnership. Accepting these types of imperfections are part of what having a mature relationship is all about (be it physical flaws, annoying habits or quirks, etc.). In contrast, deal-breakers are almost always the result of macro issues. The paradox is, macro issues are always *made up of* micro ones. So, as previously discussed, the trick is to determine whether or not the small things in question are part of a larger pattern, and if so, whether it's one you can live with. If it is a pattern, you'll know it, because it will come up often enough to be noticeable; in other words, you won't be able to miss it, because it will consistently *bother you*.

If I could give only one tip in this area that would be a particularly accurate (though not very scientific) guide to follow, it would be: **trust your instincts**. If you have an uneasy "feeling" about some aspect of a potential partner's behavior, it's probably there for a legitimate reason. You are almost certainly picking up on some real part of who that person is. In this way, human beings (even those that may not seem very bright) are amazingly perceptive. I can't tell you how often people do initially take note of this type of information, only to later discount it. For instance, a male client recently told me that on his very first date with his (recently ex) wife, he noticed that her apartment was obviously messy. Looking back, he suddenly realized: "I could plainly see that she wasn't a neat freak like me. I should have been saying to myself, 'Me and this girl got issues'." Now, fifteen years or so later, they ended up divorced largely due to that specific but *fundamental* difference. If we could more easily recognize this pattern, a lot of unnecessary heartache could be spared.

Having said this, since we *all* have our faults, we of course will all have to ultimately choose someone with *some* of these less desirable traits. So, I'm not saying that the presence of Jars in a partner is a problem in and of itself—just **which** ones and **how much** of them. What is their "degree" and "nature"? Are there any that are deal-breakers? Do they seem relatively benign? Are they workable; is the person willing and able to adjust them? These are telling but often not easy questions to answer, so again, *trust your instincts.*

Apropos of that, there's another "dual reality" to this whole selection process, which can be thought of as "the big picture" vs. "the little picture" (the nitty-gritty of everyday life). Among the masses of couples in the world, there's a subset of people who have just basically *found* "the right one." It's something that essentially happened *to them*, naturally, without all that much thought or analysis. Every individual has his or her own, for lack of a better way to put it, "relationship path," and some people are fortunate enough to have a path that leads to the right mate relatively early in life, without a lot of effort or struggle. Exactly what controls this process, or what separates those who do from those who don't, is not totally clear. If you personally have any sort of belief in some type of higher power, or order to the universe, then it could be argued that the big picture, the overall "process," is influenced by forces beyond our direct control, whereas the little picture is controlled by us and our Invisible Connection(s). Put another way, there's an element of "fate" in two people being *brought together*, but what they do *with it* is up to them and their own conscious/unconscious dynamics (e.g., pursue the relationship or not, invest further or break up, etc.).

I've heard many amazing stories of how people initially met in some seemingly "random" way and eventually ended up getting married. One of the funniest is as follows: two strangers (one male, one female) meet in an elevator at work, and are apparently attracted to each other. They spontaneously decide to go out to lunch. While on their date, they discover that they really don't have all that much in common, and it becomes obvious they're not going to go out again, but somehow they get on the subject of the tallest people they know (he has a tall male friend, she has a tall female friend). For some inexplicable reason, they decide that their tall friends should be fixed up, so they exchange phone numbers of the two people involved. Later, they both go to their tall friend, and say something like, "Here's the number of a tall man/woman," to which they both respond essentially, "What, are you crazy? I don't even know this person, and what's more, neither do *you!*"

Several months later, the woman is looking through some papers on her desk, and comes across this unknown tall guy's number. She figures, "What the heck?" so she calls him. His mother answers the phone, to which the woman identifies herself as the son's friend, and tries to leave a message. Unfortunately, the son was on vacation for a period of time, and the mother detected something fishy and said, "Well, if you really were a friend of my son's, then you'd know he's out of town." Finally, the tall woman says, "Look, Mrs. So-and-so, I'm not really your son's friend—in fact, I don't even know him, but (yada yada) and gave me his number. Just tell him if he wants to, he can call me when he gets back." Well, for some reason he decided to call her, and they've been happily married for ten years with two beautiful kids. Go figure.

Apparently, there seems to be some truth to the expression, "For every pot, there's a lid." I have heard enough real-life stories of happy couples to see a clear pattern emerge, which is, as simplistic as it may sound, "When the right one comes along, you'll know it." It seems that the "trick" is simply to be willing to *wait* until that happens—this is the big picture. However, in the nitty-gritty of everyday life, people get lonely, and they get scared ("what if I never find someone?"), and therefore frequently settle for someone who's not who they truly want. As understandable as this is, the result is that they essentially end up sidetracking their own relationship path, the one that, if they had just continued to follow, would have eventually led to their genuine partner. As you can see, this could require a great deal of patience, depending on the individual.

Why does this come sooner for some people than it does for others? I believe it's simply because they're *ready*—for the commitment of marriage or partnership, and all that goes with it. For the people fortunate enough to get this gift earlier in life, this is where the work begins, because all relationships (even right ones) require work to keep them happy, healthy, and growing. Thus, they must still deal with the nitty-gritty aspects of everyday life, which is where their Invisible Connection and Jar-related issues come into play.

This raises an interesting paradox about the Invisible Connection itself, which is that, in some ways, it's really not invisible! In other words, the pieces of the puzzle that we need to see, we actually do see; the real problem is what we *do* with that information. What then is *truly* invisible are the **under-lying forces** that tend to make us act in certain maladaptive ways. Thus, there are two basic areas in which the Invisible Connection plays itself out: in the **selection** of a relationship, and in the **carrying out** of a relationship. Both of these are actually *behavioral* in nature, meaning that they involve choices, decisions, and reactions. It is in these behaviors that we tend to be pushed and pulled by our Invisible Connections and our Jars.

Some people will have particular difficulty with the selection aspect of the Invisible Connection, and will struggle for a while to find a compatible mate, whereas others (as referenced earlier) will have a relatively easy time with it. Whether it's a smooth or bumpy path to a stable relationship, people end up in relatively the same place, which is that they will still have the ongoing challenge of carrying out their partnership in a fruitful manner. Here, the forces of the Invisible Connection will cause normally happy couples to get irritated, angry, hurt, be stubborn, and otherwise struggle to meet their own and each other's needs in a mutually satisfying way. One happily married woman, while commenting on this process, noted that couples tend to argue over only a few broad but very common themes: money, family, and sex. I would respectfully propose that underneath these (and possibly a few other) major issues that sum up the experience of partnership, there are always **principles**, or Jars, providing the fuel. The tools to more effectively manage that fuel will be addressed in Chapter Four.

When Choosing a Partner, Reality Is Your Friend

As indicated earlier, there's no such thing as a "failed relationship," only one that has been poorly selected. Contrary to what many people believe, there truly is **no such thing as**

"rejection," at least not when it comes to partnerships. If a proposition is made is for a casual dating relationship, or for a short-term sexual encounter, then yes, it is possible to be "rejected" on the basis of your looks, your personality, your job, or your car. But if the goal is for a healthy, happy, successful, and lifelong partnership, then there's no such thing as rejection. **You cannot "lose" a person who truly wants you**.

Think about that for a moment—let it settle in. By definition, a "healthy, happy, successful, and lifelong partnership" cannot occur unless the couple possesses the right combination of ingredients to make the relationship work. No matter how hard we may try, **we cannot fool reality**; the truth will eventually always catch up. If the person truly wants you, there's nothing that could cause them to (ultimately) let you go; if they don't want you, there's nothing that will (ultimately) make them stay. Therefore, *all information* that you get about your realistic chances for longterm compatibility is welcome information, even if it's *unpleasant*.

Again, if the goal is *healthy, happy, successful, and lifelong partnership*, **you'll eventually find out anyway** (whether you were well matched enough or not). There are no relation ships that are "supposed" to work out that don't. As much as it may hurt, or *feel* like a rejection at the time, the person is really just answering one bottom line question for you: "Are you 'the one' for me?" Disappointing as it may seem at that moment, if the answer is "no," it's information you're much better off knowing sooner rather than later (unless your goal is an unhappy, unhealthy relationship or divorce). One of the best defenses against making *bad* choices is making *informed* choices. So, pleasant or unpleasant, what you want to hear or not, the more realistic information you can gather, the more effective your choices will be **in the long run**.

Probably the best tip I can offer that will allow you to

"assist" reality in its ability to work for you is this: **the best way to get the *wrong* partner is to be anything other than your true self during the *entire* dating process**. I realize this is contrary to what society (and television and movies) has taught you, i.e., to try to put your "best foot forward." The problem with that approach is, you then have to live up to the version of yourself you've put out there, and if it's not who you really are (nor who you're comfortable being), then eventually it's going to catch up with you. Bottom line to this concept is **truth in advertising**. Essentially, you'll get *exactly* what you advertise for. By being genuine, you will allow the naturally occurring process of the other person's realistic reactions to you to take place in a reliable manner. The more you try to "misrepresent" yourself, the more you (perhaps unintentionally) subvert this process. As tempting as it is to try to "get" someone to like you in the short run, it most likely won't help you to find your *true* partner, in the long run.

One of the consequences of "nontotally truthful advertising" (and also one of the sadder realities of the dating world) is what could be described as an "almost" relationship. This is the one that in many *ways feels* so right, yet just doesn't seem to work out successfully. This is often a particularly painful and frustrating experience to go through, because the feelings are so strong and positive in so many ways. Because this type of relationship can appear to be the "right one," it often lingers for a long time before the couple finally comes to grips with the fact that it isn't going to work. On the other hand, as someone wise once told me, "Relationships can either be bridges or a final destination." In this sense, every relationship is very valuable, because each provides genuine practice for you to learn what you, on your own relationship path, need to know. Assuming you utilize this information in the most conscious way you're able to, you'll never lose that information, and can therefore use it repeatedly to inform all subsequent relation-ships; thus, every one of your "practice relationships" is truly a "gift that keeps on giving."

Of course, being human, it's usually not easy (nor painless) to recognize that a relationship is intended as a bridge and not as a final destination. There's an aspect to successful relation-ships that seems to resemble a "lock and key." I really don't know whether there's one single person who's "meant" for another person, or rather, a number of people who could potentially be "right ones," depending on timing, circumstance, etc. Regardless, the lock and key metaphor is a useful one, because the key either *opens* the lock or it doesn't. However, it's possible for a key to be a close enough match so that it fits into the lock, even smoothly, but simply doesn't open it. For two people to seemingly be compatible enough to have the lock and key fit together smoothly, yet not open, is pretty disap-pointing. However, painful as it may be at the time, it's also offering those individuals the information they need (if they're paying attention) to find a partner with whom they can be genuinely happy.

Chapter Four

How to Enjoy the Right One

Change Is Difficult, But the Right Tools Can Help

The areas in which couples have their greatest frustrations with each other are also the areas in which they have some of their richest opportunities to grow together, to make mutually beneficial changes in themselves and the relationship. Understanding the Invisible Connection provides the basis for many specific, systematic tools that can be used to effectively change patterns of communication between partners, as well as to improve the overall intimacy and quality of a couple's relationship. Clients frequently ask me if there's any particular thing they should look for in a partner, something that will reliably predict the relationship's potential success. I tell them that, if forced to pick only one thing, it would be **the degree to which that person is willing to make the effort to stretch and grow**. This would apply for both themselves as individuals as well as for the relationship.

As has been described throughout this text, there are many wonderful and highly functional relationships out there. I've known many couples who would genuinely fit the definition of "soulmates." One such couple exemplified the type of conscious, consistent effort that it takes to keep a marriage fresh. As a part of their everyday routine, they take time out of their busy schedules to purposefully stop and remind each other of their commitment to one another and to their life of ongoing mutual growth (they normally do this at least two to three times a day). They actually take time out to *appreciate* one another. While this may not be typical, it offers a glimpse of what's possible when people are truly willing to work at their relationship.

While we can't control our backgrounds, our childhood, our basic personality, or our Jars, we *can control* what we do *with* them. We may not be able to change who we fundamentally are, but we can do the best that's possible with what we have. People frequently ask, "Can I get rid of (or reduce) my Jars?" For the most part, the answer is "no," although it may be possible to "shave off" some portion of them. However, as one very astute friend of mine noted, a person has almost unlimited ability to expand *themselves* in order to make more room for their (and their partner's) Jars.

So, while tools usually can't eliminate problems, they can be used to significantly reduce or improve them. This is true for all three varieties of fundamentally compatible (but normally imperfect) relationships: those whose issues tend to result primarily in **conflict**, those whose issues tend to result primarily in a **loss of need-meeting**, or those whose issues result in some **combination** of the two. In any case, one of the most fundamental communication tools you can use is to **pause and think** before speaking. This seems so obvious that it's often overlooked, and therefore isn't actually applied. Like any tool that's highly effective if used properly but is sitting in the garage gathering dust, it will only be of value when utilized. As one female client noted, "It's amazing what a difference it makes when you think before reacting!" The reason this is such a crucial step is that many of our reactions, especially those that involve irritation, anger, frustration, or hurt feelings, are *automatic*. An automatic reaction requires no thought; there is no actual *choice* involved, and therefore, the amount of **control** that we have over that reaction is zero. Obviously, control is one of the ingredients necessary for a constructive discussion. When thought is introduced into the automatic process, it ceases to be automatic. Therefore, your message can be presented in a more productive manner, one which your partner will be more likely to hear. It sounds so simple, yet it's often difficult to do, because when intense emotions are involved, thinking tends to take a backseat.

This is where the second tool comes into play. Because the feelings involved are real, the trick is not so much to eliminate them as much as it is to manage them. This basically involves taking existing feelings and **redistributing** them in a more accurate and productive manner. The term I use for this technique is "**The 30/70 Split**," which refers to the fact that our reactions are partly due to immediate events and partly due to our pre-existing areas of sensitivity. The 30/70 Split provides a clear and concise reminder of which is which; approximately 30% of the total reaction is about what just happened, while the other 70% is the result of childhood feelings, or Jars, being activated.

I cannot overemphasize how crucial it is to be able to *remember this fact in the heat of an argument.* It all makes perfect sense when you read it, and then your partner pushes your buttons, and all logic goes out the window. When their Jars are opened up, human beings have an extremely reliable tendency to revert to the brain functioning of a child. Normally calm, happy, rational people can immediately become worked up, upset, or clouded when certain feelings are provoked. In many ways they literally go from being guided by their twenty-seven- or forty-five-year-old brain to being ruled by the brain of a six-year-old. As you may have noticed, operating on raw emotion rarely results in an effective discussion (nor does pure reasoning without the expression of feelings).

Maintaining this tricky balance is not at all easy to do. Therefore it's helpful to have an "arsenal" of tools at your disposal, especially ones that can quickly and easily be used to remind you to **pause and think** before reacting, yet don't result in your bottling up even more feelings. The 30/70 Split is a crucial part of this process; it emphasizes that 100% of your feelings are real, but only about 30% of them are due to your partner's actions. The problem is, we are extremely prone to slamming our partner with the full 100% instead of the 30 that they've earned. People can usually tolerate a 30% reaction, but can rarely tolerate a 100% reaction. The most difficult part of using this tool effectively is that your brain will persistently try to convince you that your feelings are all about your *partner's* actions and little or nothing to do with your previous experiences, your childhood, or your parents. This is a problem, because if you believe that your partner is *the problem* (as opposed to the *trigger* for the problem), then, of course, you'd naturally try to fix and or change *them*. Meanwhile, in actuality, the bulk of the real problem is still going unaddressed, because it was **already there long before you ever met your partner**.

To help you to better understand the 30/70 Split, here are a number of metaphors for the way in which the full 100% of feelings are actually made up of two separate (but related) parts:

30%	70%
situation	Jar
present	past
salt	wound
messenger	message
spark	fuel
trigger	mechanism
tip	emotional iceberg
tree	forest
detail	pattern
outlet	reservoir

Some Examples

My wife said she'd be home by 7 and it's now 8 and she hasn't called	Consideration
My husband went to watch a football game with his friends and left me home to watch the kids	Availability
My girlfriend frequently misplaces her keys and then frantically asks me to help her find them	Irrationality
My boyfriend makes joking comments about me in front of our friends	Respect
When we cook together, my husband will often tell me the "proper" way in which to do my part	Control
When I do bill paying or other household chores, my wife points out any errors that I've made	Criticism
When I try to get my husband to understand what I'm saying, he says, "I know, I know!"	Closed-mindedness

In each of these cases, there are **actual situations** to deal with that would naturally provoke a certain level of **real feelings** for most people. But when you notice that you or your partner has an *intense reaction*, it's **a dead giveaway that a Jar has just been opened up** (the situation acts as a "jar opener"). Notice that I'm not calling this "The 5/95 Split," which would indicate that your partner's actions had almost no reality to them, and that your reaction was all about you and your issues. That's not true—people actually do *real* behaviors that have a *real* impact on us. So, the trick is to confront your partner only with the portion of the problem that they have "earned" (approximately 30%). To use another metaphor, **don't pin the tail on the wrong donkey**. Of course, you still have to find something constructive to do with the *right* donkey, which is the other 70%, and that (unfortunately) may mean having to spend some time with unpleasant childhood feelings. In a sense, this is akin to "mourning," and involves similar methods of processing feelings, such as reflection (thinking and feeling), crying, physical expression (exercise), verbalizing (to yourself or others), and writing.

If You Never Fight, You're Abnormal

Consistent recognition and use of the 30/70 Split helps to maintain relative peace in the day-to-day existence of the relationship, and points to another technique, which is to establish a mutual objective to allow **flare-ups instead of blow-ups**. Many people have the idea that a successful relationship is one in which the participants do not fight...this is false. The key is learning to fight *well*. This means allowing each person the chance to honestly express thoughts and feelings and yet avoid tearing each other to shreds in the process; again, a delicate balance. The crucial difference between a flare-up and a blow-up is acting on what I call a **Surge of Energy**. This is the sensation (heat, pressure, tightness) that you get in your stomach, chest, face, etc., when your buttons get pushed; you experience an immediate, rapid rise in emotional intensity, which usually results in a strong expression of feelings, verbal or otherwise. It may be obvious that the words that come out of a person's mouth in these moments do not tend to be very productive; they are usually angry, mean, harsh, critical, accusatory, or generally hurtful. In turn, the other person's "Surge of Energy" is activated, producing similar results, and so on. This is a surefire recipe for a blow-up. As with the 30/70 Split, the Surge of Energy is a dead giveaway that a Jar has been opened up, and that a heat-seeking missile has been launched.

The difference between a blow-up and a flare-up is what a person does with his or her Surge of Energy. That these surges will occur is a given; the option of preventing them entirely is not one that's available to the human race. Therefore, the problem is not so much *that* they occur, but our responses *when* they occur. The most normal response is **action** (thereby allowing the heat-seeking missile to hit its target); the goal is to learn to consistently replace action with a **pause**. Although the surge rises quickly, it will also fall quickly if given the chance. If people did this as a general rule—paused before speaking or reacting—the world would be a different place. Once the pause is introduced, the person can speak in a relatively constructive manner, as opposed to spewing raw emotion. As one client accurately put it, "The goal is to use the Surge of Energy as a dimmer switch." The result is *communication*; maybe with some irritation, maybe with some frustration or anger, but communication will occur...a flare-up, not a blow-up.

The Effectiveness of the Tools
Equals the Use of the Tools

The ability to move reasonably smoothly through most conflicts without becoming bogged down rarely occurs by itself; it's a skill, and therefore takes much practice and the use of reliable techniques. Many of the techniques are variations on a similar theme, but most are designed to help a person to catch themselves *prior* to reacting automatically. That's the pivotal step; **automatic reactions are the enemy of free choice**. The Surge of Energy is the most immediately effective tool in this process; it is your "ace in the hole," a **red flag** that alerts you that one of your Jars has just been activated, and that it's time to pause and think. The more quickly and reliably someone can remember to do this, the more likely he or she will be to avoid knee-jerk reactions (which tend to be inherently destructive). On the other hand, a conscious or *thoughtful* response can allow you to say something constructive, something you actually need or want to communicate.

This introduces another technique: "**say what you mean, and mean what you say**." Ironically, although it's a common enough expression to be a cliché, people rarely actually do it. It's amazing how helpful this approach can be in effectively communicating your wishes to your partner...*say what you mean, and mean what you say*. One of the major obstacles to this level of communication is the need that people have to prove their point to their partner. This is that fundamental desire for mastery, and while it is normal, it often produces unwanted results. The trick is to get our point across without the nasty side-effects. It turns out that in any argument, there are actually two discussions rolled up together; the issue that you want your partner to understand (30%), and the issue you want your *parents* (and all previous transgressors) to understand (70%). Because of the truly deep need for mastery involved in the parents' portion, it's very easy to end up in a dead-end discussion with your partner. We tend to get caught up in the principle of *winning*, in which the primary goal shifts from: (1) asking your partner to make a desirable adjustment in his or her behavior, to: (2) converting him or her to your way of thinking, or: (3) acting out "revenge" for a lifetime's worth of accumulated frustration over this issue. It's no longer about the original issue; now they actually have to **agree** with you (often an unattainable goal).

People commonly have heated arguments over everyday details: "How many times have I asked you to dump out the coffee grinds after you make coffee?! It gets moldy!!!" Your point may in fact be valid; the question is, how much have you gained? Is it worth hurting your partner over coffee grounds or donuts? The "solution" to this stalemate is often found in one's ability to give up on the principle of winning, or proving your point. On the other hand, it's equally damaging to get in the habit of stifling your thoughts and feelings. A compromise solution to this dilemma is to simply state your point to the other person **for the record**. The goal of this approach is not necessarily to get the other person to agree with you, but rather to provide yourself with a means of expression. While you may not have achieved total victory, you'll still be able to get your point across. However, in order for this technique to be fully effective, a couple has to have agreed to use it, preferably ahead of time. This allows them easy access to it thereafter, sort of a "shorthand" with each other: "You don't have to agree with me, but I'm just letting you know, *for the record*."

In addition, "say what you mean and mean what you say" is often easier said than done. It requires that you manage your feelings well enough to clearly and accurately state, as much as possible, what you really want your partner to know. This is usually either a request for them to make some kind of actual behavioral change, or simply a means for you to communicate your own thoughts or feelings about a particular issue. In the case of asking for behavioral change(s), you may want them to **stop doing something** ("please stop leaving your shoes in the middle of the floor"), **start doing something** ("if you're going to be more than a half-hour late, can you please call?"), or **adjust something they're already doing** ("when I ask you a question, could you give me a more definite answer?").

Phrases like "you always ____," "you never ____," "I hate it when you ____," "why do you have to be so ____," etc., have no constructive place in genuine communication, because they're rarely fully accurate, but rather are *exaggerations*. Similarly, markedly raised voices, silence, curses, or other types of insulting or inflammatory language tend to defeat your purpose. When this method is used to express your point, even if it's a legitimate one, your partner is likely to react more to the *method* than the *information*. Although the urge to simply *vent* feelings at your partner is both normal and understandable, it generally won't get you what you really want, which is for them to make some attempt at honoring your wishes.

However, since the need that we have to express our feelings is so deep, stating things "for the record" provides an effective, yet undamaging, outlet. Examples:

1. "It's not that you're really doing anything wrong, but it does hurt my feelings when you don't call me right back."
2. "I know that you have your own method, but it irritates me that you consistently misplace your keys."
3. "I know it's not that big of a deal, but it kind of makes me feel unimportant when you watch TV while I'm talking to you."
4. "Maybe your way of making this recipe is more precise, but I

prefer to just do it the way that I'm used to doing it."
5. "I know that you're angry, but when you yell at me it just makes me shut down."

Stating things for the record allows you to register a complaint without creating a blowup, while at the same time planting a "seed" for future reference.

The Three Jars—Your Personal Road Map to Irritation

Throughout this book, the concept of people's "issues" has come up repeatedly. As previously discussed, the tool that's the most pivotal is **The Three Jars Technique**. Most of the techniques presented require a person to know what his or her issues are. The more immediately available that information is, the more quickly and effectively it can be utilized. The "Three Jars" provides a simple method to obtain this information about yourself and your partner. The more familiar you both are with your Jars, the more effectively you'll be able to apply them to the **language** of your relationship. For instance, one client reported a situation (thereafter known as "The Sponge Incident") in which the husband said to the wife, "Where's the sponge?" She responded angrily, "I don't know where the _____ sponge is!"

This is the moment that the vast majority of arguments are either created or diffused, the difference between a flare-up and a blow-up. Because of the force of her reaction, *he* was naturally tempted to give an equally strong response back. However, at that second it registered with him that he felt a Surge of Energy; he also then realized that her reaction must have been the result of one as well. Suddenly, it hit him; "Oops, I guess I opened one of her Jars." While pausing and thinking, he hears the tone that he had used when asking, "Where's the sponge," and realizes that it had kind of an accusatory edge to it. "Ah-ha! That's her father. That's that 'criticism Jar.'"

Upon this moment of insight, his Surge of Energy gave way to understanding. Given that he really did love his wife, and that he knew that her criticism Jar was a source of genuine pain for her, his initial reaction of defensiveness and anger quickly softened. It's very important when using these tools to make a conscious effort to **remember why you chose to marry this person in the first place**; presumably, because you truly loved and appreciated them. With all of the unconscious, invisible, dysfunctional stuff involved, there are still plenty of conscious, visible, and healthy reasons for you and your partner to be together and enjoy one another.

One of the most common barriers to couples (and people) understanding one another is that, when something bothers *you*, the fact that it *should* bother you is obvious, whereas when something bothers *someone else*, it often seems unreasonable. This phenomenon is easy to explain; **you know that your sensitive spots are sensitive to you**. When your own buttons get pushed, it immediately makes sense why ("Well, duh, that would bother anyone!"), but when your partner over-reacts, you may think, "I don't get it." This clarifies an important aspect of a couple's ability to communicate effectively: your partner's issues are just as painful to them as yours are to you. It probably won't instinctively *feel* that way to you, assuming it's not your Jar, but it will to them (just as they may not be equally disturbed by something that would bother you). This is where empathy can be helpful, which essentially means to see (and feel) things from *their* point of view instead of your own. It also provides an opportunity to actually change the language of your relationship, as well as show your partner that you're paying attention ("Oops, sorry, I didn't mean to open up your guilt Jar," or "You are really irritating my fairness Jar!"). You'd be amazed how just *naming something* can help you to diffuse many a situation.

I Thought I Knew Why This Was Bothering Me, But...

One of the things that commonly interferes with the enjoyment of a relationship is the ongoing, nagging kind of disagreements and irritations that are just a normal part of the process when two or more people are together. Often, certain things that your partner does will cause you some kind of discomfort, but it may not be apparent why. In cases when you find yourself having a particularly strong reaction, it is usually wise to say to yourself, "Hmm—something else must be going on here." In order to accurately distinguish between your own pre-existing issues and the actions of your partner, there are two simple tools that you can use. The first is called **Connect the Dots**, and it works as follows (see tool sheet, next page): in the upper dot, write a brief, one sentence description that captures the *gist* of your complaint. In the lower dot, simply identify which one (or more) of your Jars best describes the principle being violated in the first dot. Then, just connect the dots! If you're using the tool correctly, you should find yourself saying, "Ah-ha...now I know why this is bothering me *so much*."

Connect the Dots

Situation/Complaint

1) (wife leaves coffee grounds) "Why can't she just remember a simple request?"

2) (girlfriend misplaces car keys) "But it's so easy to put them in the same place—it doesn't make any sense!"

3) (husband says, "Where's the sponge?") "Why are you assuming that *I'm* the one who misplaced it?"

Jar(s)/Principle

1) inconsideration

2) irrationality

3) criticism or guilt

The second technique is called **The Room Transfer**. This will help you if you're having trouble seeing the connection between your partner's behavior and your (possibly hidden) issue with your parent(s). It's particularly useful when a situation is *persistently* bothering you, but you can't figure out why. In a sentence or two, state your fundamental complaint with your partner's actions. Leave your partner's "room," close the door, go across the hall, and enter either your mother's or father's "room." State the exact same complaint, and see if it fits; if it does, then you know where the *underlying* fuel is coming from. You'll be surprised how often this turns out to be true. This is an example of the "dual realities" in action; you're fully aware that you're complaining about something on one level (your partner's behavior), while, on another, deeper level, you're *unintentionally* also complaining about an issue with which you've had many previous negative experiences (most likely with your parents).

Many times the connection is one that may not (initially) seem at all obvious to you. For instance, the aforementioned client with the unreliable girlfriend, when venting frustration over one of her recent transgressions, made the statement, "How can she not realize that when she's not there for me, it makes me feel unwanted?" I suggested that he try the Room Transfer Technique ("I know you're talking about your girlfriend, but leave her 'room,' close the door, and go into your mother's 'room,' and make *the same exact statement.*") When he did, the light bulb went on; "Jeez . . . that's my mother." He knew he was talking about his girlfriend, **but he didn't realize he was talking about his mother as well**. Between his girlfriend and his mother, which one would have more power to hurt him? Who came first?

Again, *this is not an issue of blame*; it's about understanding **why** you feel so strongly about something, and **what** it's *really* about. **It's very difficult to fix a problem when you keep trying to fix the wrong problem**. Another client was struggling with some sexual issues in her relationship. She was describing how she often became somewhat panicky when she knew that she and her boyfriend were going to have sex. She loved him and enjoyed making love with him, so she was confused by her response. When I asked her what went through her head in these situations, she said, "Well, you know, I just feel like I have to live up to his expectation of how I'm supposed to be." Without realizing it, she was describing her relationship with her father to a tee (criticism/perfectionism Jar). It was so exact that she might as well have superimposed the words from one situation onto the other—thus the name "Room Transfer."

You might be surprised to discover how often you *think and feel* that you're talking about what your partner did, when you're also dead-on accurately describing something that your parent(s) did many times over many years ago. Here are some other examples from actual clients:

(1) "I don't know why it's bothering me so much, but I hate the idea that my ex-wife is out there just having a grand old time." (His mother was an alcoholic and often neglected the family).

(2) "I feel like you're always trying to get me to do things *your* way, and I don't get to have a say." (Her father was extremely controlling).

(3) "When I don't do something right, you act disappointed, and it makes me feel like I let you down." (His mother had high expectations and was a "guilt-tripper").

(4) "You don't tell me what you're thinking, and it makes me feel nervous, like I don't know where I stand with you." (Her father was the "strong silent type").

(5) "It seems like you find something wrong with almost every-

thing I do." (Her mother was a perfectionist).

In each of these cases, and countless others, there is some genuine complaint with the partner's behavior, but the fuel, the power, the *intensity* of the feelings has a very old and familiar ring to it. As with many of the other tools, The Room Transfer helps you **to not pin the tail on the wrong donkey**.

Change Is a Process

Equipped with the information in your **Three Jars**, you can begin to utilize the techniques described. It's a systematic and reliable set of tools, but again, the crucial step is that you must **use them**. Recently, a client inquired (regarding the issues in his Three Jars), "What's the cure?" Unfortunately, I was unable to provide an absolute answer to this question. With many medical problems, you go to the doctor and he or she actually provides the cure, whether it be in the form of medication, surgery, or some other procedure. In many cases, that's it, you're done. With psychological and emotional issues, there's no such thing as a cure, only a **process**. Your emotional and psychological makeup is a large part of *who* you are, and it's no more possible to remove those parts from your "self" than it would be to rip out the entire fifth floor of a forty story building while leaving the rest of the building intact.

We may not be able to fix or change who we are or our history, but we can make the most possible with what we have. To do this effectively, we need tools. Like all tools, in order to be fully effective, they must be used over and over again on an ongoing basis, whenever needed. For instance, buying an exercise machine does not cause you to get in shape. In fact, just buying it is of almost no value whatsoever; it's the **use** of that tool, that machine, that makes it effective, that allows you to achieve *results*. In addition, let's say you do use it regularly for six months...you're done, right? Now you're in the shape you want to be in, so you can stop. I know...it would be nice. But, with issues such as physical fitness and personal growth, there just is no "finished product." Instead, it's always more of "a work in progress," requiring ongoing attention and mainte-nance—as imperfect human beings, that's the best we can do. Having said this, we as imperfect human beings are also capable of amazing growth, and of creating deeply loving, joyful, and satisfying relationships.

Skills and tools provide the *method* to accomplish this. How do you know when to use a tool? Simple—whenever you *need* it. When do you use a food processor (if you're so inclined)? When you need to chop something. We all probably own a hammer, but we only use it when the need *presents itself*. But because feelings are involved with emotional tools, it can at times be difficult or painful to use them, and it takes some discipline to *keep* using them. Like any skill, at first they may feel awkward and somewhat unnatural, but with repeti-tion, they get easier over time. And, like many tools (such as the exercise machine), the only real limitation in their effectiveness is the user's **will** to use them. If you're willing to put forth the **effort** to use them, the tools can offer almost unlimited rewards for both you and your partner.

A couple was in my office recently, working on techniques to improve their communication. As we reviewed the steps ("whenever you feel the Surge of Energy, it's an immediate signal to pause and think"), the wife blurted out, "Well, if you pause and think, what are you supposed to do with the surge of energy?!" After we all laughed, she answered her own question (use the 30/70 Split), but it raised an important point, one that just about anyone could relate to. Controlling your impulses and redirecting them in a different and more effective manner isn't easy; it does take a certain amount of effort. After all, it's gratifying to discharge that energy; it *feels* good, at least momentarily.

The bigger question, one that each person must decide upon individually, is which response will provide the greatest benefit **overall**? Is your primary objective to slam your partner, or is it to be understood by him or her? Is it to prove that you're right so that you can gloat, or is it to maintain a loving and productive partnership? Relationships don't tend to thrive on their own, and often our natural instincts lead us toward destructive behaviors. Knowledge is the missing ingredient; it allows us to learn enough about the directions that we're pulled in automatically that we no longer *have* to go there. It's about making more informed choices, more *conscious* decisions. It's about not repeating the same mistakes. In the interest of meeting these goals, here's a condensed version of the story:

(1) Accept that the Invisible Connection is something we're all stuck with. Like it or not, we will be pulled in the direction of the blueprint provided by the negative aspects of our relationship with our parents. Since we all have to have our own version of the Invisible Connection, we might as well learn how to find a relatively benign one.

(2) A large portion of our strong reactions to our partners will really be anger, annoyance, or frustration toward our parents in disguise.

(3) The word "chemistry" is a good example of the "dual reality" of relationships. It's typically thought of as a great thing, something that indicates how "right" two people are together. However, it also means combustibility, friction, or irritation. Although the obvious subjective *feeling* may be a wonderful experience (excitement, passion), it's

a clear indication of a very powerful Invisible Connection simmering underneath.

(4) We will have a persistent and never-ending need to (at times) prove to our partners the ways in which they are wrong, stupid, inconsiderate, foolish, neglectful, or messy. This need will be partly about the actual behavior of our partner (30%), and mostly about the past behavior of our parents (70%).

(5) Our brain will consistently try to convince us that our feelings have absolutely nothing to do with our parents, and everything to do with our partner.

(6) Because of this mistaken belief, we will often find ourselves engaged in a revolving cycle of conflict, trying to get our partner to see our point of view.

(7) We *will* fight in our relationships; that's normal. Aim for flareups, not blowups.

(8) Humor is a tremendous tool. There's no one way to achieve this; it's whatever works in your relationship. Sometimes it's the goofiest thing that can diffuse a conflict enough to allow you to talk to each other. Try to develop "code language" with your partner; these are inside jokes that you can instantly use at appropriate times (I had a partner who, when she knew she had offended me, would come up behind me and timidly sniff me like a puppy. It's pretty hard to stay mad after something like that).

(9) Say what you mean and mean what you say.

(10) Get good at noticing Energy Surges quickly, before they can cause damage.

(11) Know your and your partner's Three Jars like the back of your hand. All thoughts, feelings, perceptions, reactions, and choices will be filtered through the subjective lens of a person's Jars. Make a conscious effort to build Jar awareness and terminology into the language of your rela-

tionship.

(12) Areas of blindness that we have about our parents' faults will be the same as those that we have toward our potential partners.

(13) People often mistakenly equate the amount of *feelings* they have for a person with the amount of *compatibility* they have with that person. These two issues can be highly correlated (in the right match), but they can also have almost no correlation whatsoever. In fact (per the Invisible Connection), it is possible to experience very intense and real feelings for someone largely *because* of a high degree of built-in incompatibility. The best relationships tend to be the product of both love/feelings *and* well-matched ingredients. This truth can be one of the hardest relationship lessons to learn.

(14) Try to be mindful that we're always operating on two levels simultaneously, visible and invisible (conscious and unconscious), and that the unconscious often has its own (hidden) agenda.

(15) Crucial aspects of your and your partner's unconscious agendas will be exactly opposed to one another and will therefore have the tendency to consistently irritate and frustrate you both. This is no accident; it is the Invisible Connection.

(16) Watch out for the qualities that strongly attract you to someone from the beginning—these are often the "blueprint," the early form, of what turns out to be the Invisible Connection. As one friend put it so well, "What initially attracted me eventually did me in."

(17) As simple as this sounds, it's so easy to forget...try to remember that you're (supposed to be) on the *same side*.

(18) Remember...it's all about **mastery**.

One client recently asked, "But do we ever *achieve* mastery?" The answer to this is both "yes" and "no." The mastery process is never-ending, and the sense of victory that we experience tends to be extremely temporary; for the moment, or the hour, or the day. We are continually seeking opportunities for mastery, both consciously and unconsciously, in all things that we do. To this extent, we never actually achieve mastery, and will always struggle to some degree with the Invisible Connection in our relationships.

However, it is very much possible to find a *better* version of it, a more benign version. As previously discussed, this has much to do with the personality style of the individuals involved and their particular "fit," but there are some other key indicators, such as overall temperament, open-mindedness, and especially the willingness to make an effort, to struggle with self-examination. Also, there are some aspects that don't seem to be in our direct control, whether you want to call it luck, fate, destiny, or whatever. Just to even find another person that you fundamentally *like* to such a degree is very fortunate.

Even with all of these positive elements in place, the mastery process is never *complete*. In relationships that work well, people establish a mutually beneficial "equilibrium"; they learn to **compromise**, to see each other's issues and to consciously work *with* them, to cooperate with each other. This is no easy task, because it involves what amounts to a constant degree of courage. If knowledge is power, then an open mind is a powerful mind; but it's also somewhat unprotected, and therefore vulnerable. Using these tools involves being aware of some of your own most painful issues, and being willing to share them with your partner. Although it's often difficult, and a struggle, the benefits far outweigh the costs, in the long run. Be patient.

Worksheets

Understanding Your Jars—frequently asked questions:

1) "Exactly how do I determine my Jars?"

The strict definition of how to select your Jars was described previously in the text as follows: for most of us, our parents' good qualities far outweigh their bad. With that in mind, we could probably construct a much larger list of those qualities that we love and appreciate about them. However, for *this* particular exercise, we will focus only on their less desirable qualities. Take both parents, and identify every single negative aspect of them that you can think of (for some people this is easy, for others it's quite difficult). These can consist of personality or behavior traits, attitudes, habits, lifestyle issues, beliefs, career choices, etc. Take all of those pieces of "data," big or small, and dump them all into a huge vat. Remember—we're not making value judgments or attempting to cast blame, just collecting **data**.

Now, take all of that information in the vat, and let it filter down through 100 funnels, 50 funnels, 20 funnels, until you come down to just three funnels, into Three Jars. Those Three Jars will provide you with a blueprint for just about any issue or situation in your life that you would consider to be undesirable or problematic.

2) "I can see things on this Jar list that do upset me, but I really don't think that it has anything to do with my parents. Can I have the Jar without it relating to my family?"

111

This is a tough one. The truth is, not really. Jars, by definition, are approximately 75% formed in concrete by the time a person is six years old, and 90% by the age of ten. Of course, there are many powerful, life-shaping experiences that occur after this point, but they do not create new Jars, but rather **piggyback on top of previous experiences**. In other words, the Jar itself is primarily formed in the first six years of life, and then acts as a receptacle for all subsequent experience. The question is, who is the *primary* influence for a child in the first six years of life? Clearly, it's either a parent, parents, or "parenting figures" (daycare, nanny, other family members, etc.). Either way, it still comes out basically the same. It's not so much individual moments or incidents that create Jars, but the overall *environment*. Every household has a certain theme to it, a particular *flavor*, and it is this flavor that is captured by one's Jars.

So, it's not so important that you're able to specify exactly what part of what Jar came from what experience, as much as it is to capture the collective theme, or essence, of the early period of your life. Having said this, some people have difficulty looking back and remembering these early experiences, but they have no trouble identifying the things that bug them *now*, today. In other words, another way to figure out your Three Jars is to simply look at the list and find the three issues that you know you don't like.

Almost all people will have some level of negative experience with almost all of the eighteen Jars, but certain ones will "jump out" at an individual person more than others. So, for instance, as you survey the list, you may find yourself saying, "Hmm, fairness, nah...dependability, not so much...ooh! Control! I hate it when (my boss, my spouse) tells me what to do!" Okay, go ahead and circle "control," because you clearly have the control Jar. Once you know what your three primary

Jars are, you can begin working with them. It doesn't matter as much (initially) if you understand exactly where they came from.

3) "I'm confused…is my Jar something that I don't like *when* other people do it, or is it a behavior or trait that I myself have?"

It varies. This part is not uniform among all people. The Jar is, by definition, something that bothers you when a person or situation violates that **principle** (i.e., when something is *unfair*, when someone behaves *irrationally*, when a person speaks in a *critical* tone, etc.). Therefore, the answer to the first part of the question is, yes, our Jars are **always** something that we don't like in others' behavior.

When it comes to the second part of the question, we *may* possess or display that very same characteristic ourselves, but we won't necessarily. It depends on the person. For instance, someone with a "control" Jar won't like controlling behavior in others, and in addition, may be a "control freak" themselves. People almost always go **one way or the other**. Thus, if they have the control Jar, it means they've had (too much) previous negative experience with being controlled. As a result, people will generally respond by going one way or the other—either in the **same** direction as the "bruised" area, or the **opposite**. So, the person with the control Jar will either be controlling, or very passive. The person with the guilt Jar will always be prone to *feeling* guilty; then, in addition, they may also tend to put guilt trips on others, or instead, go out of their way *not to* impose on others. The person with the anger Jar (are sensitive to other people's anger) may themselves have a harsh temper, or may have gone the other way, and therefore avoid conflict altogether. The bottom line is, your Jar is your "issue," your "sensitive spot." Your Three Jars are the building blocks of your personality, the core of who you are and your unique makeup (both strengths and weaknesses), and are therefore areas you're always vulnerable to having poked, triggered, or opened up.

A quick word on the "dual reality" of Jars. As mentioned, they contain the essence of who we are, both "good" and "bad." **There is absolutely no shame in having Jars**. The concept is one that provides you with invaluable **data** in order to better understand yourself, and your reactions, choices, and behavior. Jars can go in a variety of directions, and they take many forms, shapes and sizes. For instance, some of the nicest, most thoughtful people around may have a "dependability" Jar. As a result, they're very reliable, and are wonderful people to have as friends. On the other hand, hanging around with someone who's a perfectionist can be pretty irritating at times. But does that mean it's a "bad" trait? If you were having open-heart surgery, can you imagine having a surgeon who's not a perfectionist? Clearly, what's contained in our Jars is valuable, powerful material—the key is knowing what's *in them*, so we're better able to **manage** who we are.

Narrowing Down Your Jars

There are some simple tips on helping you to narrow your Jars down to three. A lot of people look at the list and say, "Well, I've got, like, *ten* of these!" That's normal—all of the Jars are just universal life **principles**; they are simply part of the human experience. While you may be able to *relate* to many of them, it's useful to try to narrow them down to three or four. From a practical standpoint, this allows you to make use of the tools most effectively, because you have just those three "labels" to keep track of and work with. So, try to pick the ones that you would consider to be "killer" (as opposed to just mildly annoying).

A key element of the concept of a "Jar" is that they can vary in size. Some Jars will be bigger than others, and smaller ones can actually fit into bigger ones (in other words, some of your sensitive issues, from a practical standpoint, are actually just *part of* other, bigger issues). For example, if someone has the "self-esteem" Jar, then it would be reasonable that the person might be upset if one of their friends cancelled plans at the last minute ("dependability"). In this case, the person may not have an actual dependability Jar, but instead, the *real* issue is that the friend's behavior resulted in hurting their *feelings*. In other words, the change in plans, for this particular person, was a blow to their ego—it opened up their self-esteem Jar. Other examples (of smaller Jars fitting into larger ones):

- (lack of) attention, affection, and expression are all related— pick only one. In addition, they are all "smaller" versions of both "availability" and "loss." Therefore, if you have either of these two, you don't need to pick any of the "lack of" Jars, because they are *already covered* by the bigger one (avail- ability or loss).
- Avoid choosing Jars that, although they may have a different "flavor," also obviously overlap (i.e., fairness, respect, and consideration; control and closed-mindedness/rigidity, etc.).
- When in doubt, always try to go with the Jar that seems to you to be dominant, i.e., it's irrational when people do things that are unequal or unfair, but which issue burns you up the most, fairness, or irrationality? If people are untrustworthy or unloyal, they may end up leaving the relationship. To

you (given your history), which is worse—suffering a loss, or dealing with the fact that someone lied?

Two final points on selecting your Jars. **The exact contents of a particular Jar can vary from person to person, but the gist is still basically the same**. In other words, generally speaking, a control Jar is a control Jar; a guilt Jar is a guilt Jar; a passivity Jar is a passivity Jar. Your parent(s) could have been super-loving and therefore "over-protective," or could have been mean and bossy—**either way**, it still adds up to basically the same Jar (control). Remember, this is not a value judgment, a criticism, or an issue of blame. It's understanding the *essence* of the influences that shaped who you are. If you were "controlled," whether gently and subtly, or harshly and overtly, you will still be sensitive to that particular issue.

Now, of course, Jars can be somewhat different in their *intensity* (what you could think of as "bigger" or "smaller" ones, or *how much* is in them), but the **basic contents** will still be essentially the same. A good way to look at it is as if they were "cookie Jars." You could have a variety of specific types of cookies in there—chocolate chip, oatmeal raisin, and Oreos. From a very concrete viewpoint, you could say they're all *different*—two have chocolate, but only one has cream, and the other has no chocolate or cream. But from a broader perspective, **they're all just cookies**. If they're in that particular cookie Jar (criticism, respect, availability, etc.), then it's the essence of that Jar that counts. Try not to get too caught up in the semantics of the terminology. Remember—the whole point of the Jar concept is that it's not so much the *details* that are crucial as much as the broad themes, or principles. What's most important is that you are able to capture *your themes*. It doesn't much matter what I or anybody else would call your

Jar...it's what makes sense to you that ultimately allows the concept to be useful. If there's a fairly intense and *meaningful* feeling to you about a particular Jar, even if you're not exactly sure why or how, then it's letting you know that it's a fruitful issue for you to pay closer attention to.

Lastly, it's normal for it to take some time for a person to ultimately decide which are their most genuine "Three Jars." Of course, there's really no right or wrong about this anyway, no "grading system." The value of the Three Jars Technique is that it gives you clear, relevant labels for you to be able to quickly understand your thoughts, feelings, reactions, and choices. You can begin using these labels immediately; if you eventually realize that another one is better suited to you, then you just switch labels. One question that will usually clear up any possible confusion is this: "Is this an issue that consistently and noticeably bothers me?" If it is, it's almost certainly one of your Jars. Give the concept, and the use of it as a tool, a chance to grow and develop over time. You will likely find that you'll continually discover new meaning in your own Three Jars as you become more familiar with them.

Relationship Pies

There are two versions of the "relationship pie"—macro and micro. The macro pie is made up of only seven slices, but they are all huge in importance. They represent the most basic elements of a relationship. There's no precise way to measure how much of the pie is "enough," but two-thirds to three quarters would seem to be a good guideline.

The micro pie consists of the features listed on pages 67-69. These items largely represent tastes or preferences, and as such are highly subjective to each individual. Clearly, it would be unrealistic to expect to find another person who has all these qualities, so the two-thirds/three quarters standard again seems appropriate. Simply put, it means you wouldn't get *everything* you desire in a partner, but they would still possess significantly more of what you do want than what you don't. Each individual must decide for him or herself exactly which ingredients are most important, and just what "weight" to give to those items. Remember, this is not meant as a precise formula, nor as something to be used as a shield to prevent you from openly engaging in the dating process, nor as a means of not seeing people for who they really are. Rather, it is intended as a *tool*, to allow you to:

- Increase your consciousness of the process and what you're looking for
- Pay attention to what you truly want and need in a partner-ship
- Help turn invisible into visible

Macro pie:

(1) Mind—overall intelligence, thinking style, education, depth
(2) Body—physical attraction, sexual compatibility
(3) Heart—emotional style and makeup, depth of feelings and sensitivity
(4) Soul—spirituality, philosophy, religion
(5) Common goals—career, work-life balance, family, financial/material
(6) Everyday compatibility—"getting along," lifestyle, cooperation, communication
(7) Invisible Connection—relatively benign, workable

Micro pie:

(1)   interests (hobbies, tastes)

(2)   lifestyle ("speed" of life, i.e., casual, fast-paced, hard-driving, night or morning)

(3)   values (priorities, beliefs, commitment to growth)

(4)   emotional style (warm, open, sensitive, empathic, cool, defensive, stoic, intolerant)

(5)   intellectual style (level of intelligence, complex or simple, esoteric or concrete)

(6)   energy level (hyper vs. needs a lot of sleep)

(7)   personal habits (rigid or flexible, quirky or not, high or low maintenance)

(8)   motivation level (willingness to try, put forth effort)

(9)   problem-solving style (active or passive, systematic or random, internal or external)

(10) career orientation (work to live or live to work, employee or entrepreneur)

(11) social style (gregarious or private, introvert or extrovert)

(12) approaches to diet and fitness (way of life, casual interest, etc.)

(13) verbal style (talkative, expressive, quiet, reserved)

(14) sexual appetites and preferences (frequency, wild or conservative, etc.)

(15) physical appearance (low priority, obsession, etc.)

(16) sense of humor (dry, silly, consistent, occasional)

(17) attitude (positive, negative, hopeful, pessimistic)

(18) financial goals (money/possessions as major priority, just want enough to live, etc.)

(19) spiritual or philosophical viewpoints (deep and explorative, surface and tangible)

(20) religious orientation (type, practicing or not, etc.)

(21) political views (liberal, conservative, socially conscious, self-oriented)

(22) temperament (uptight or easy-going, snuggly or squirmy, needy or self-reliant, loud or quiet)

(23) family orientation (kids—yes or no, how many, who will raise them)

(24) couple orientation (closeness vs. distance, shared time vs. independent activity)

(25) cooperation (willingness, ability, mutual or one-sided, comfort/easiness)

About the Author

Jeff Auerbach, Psy.D.

Dr. Jeff Auerbach received his Doctor of Psychology degree in clinical psychology from Widener University in 1994. His dissertation was entitled "Psychological and Emotional Issues in the World of Men's Sports."

Upon completion of his training, Dr. Auerbach worked in a variety of settings with a broad range of clients and issues, including anxiety, depression, work stress and performance, and relationships. He worked for a number of years in the community mental health system treating chronically mentally ill patients. Dr. Auerbach has also worked with thousands of everyday, successful people (also known as "the worried well") in a number of outpatient settings, including EAP work with employees from companies such as MBNA America, Bank One, the United Stated Postal Service, Astra-Zeneca, Fed-Ex, and UPS.

Dr. Auerbach's primary specialty is helping people to identify and modify extremely common, though ineffective, patterns of behavior. Through years of research, he has developed an original format (called "The Three Jars Technique") that concretely breaks down the eighteen issues or "buttons" of the human condition (i.e., principles such as fairness, control, or guilt). Through the use of this tool, Dr. Auerbach helps clients to systematically identify the (typically three) core issues that are the building blocks of their own personality. With this simple blueprint, a client is able to modify virtually any situation in their life that they would consider to be undesirable, including thoughts, feelings, reactions, choices, work performance, and all types of relationships.

Dr. Auerbach is currently in private practice. He does outpatient counseling with individuals and couples, and conducts workshops for a wide variety of clients, including relationship seminars for couples, as well as "Irritation Management" workshops for numerous public and private organizations and corporations.

Dr. Auerbach can be contacted at:
www.irritationmanagement.com

Notes

Notes

Notes

Notes

Notes

Notes